The Economic Consequences of Rolling Back the Welfare State

Munich Lectures in Economics
Edited by Hans-Werner Sinn

The Making of Economic Policy: A Transaction-Cost Politics Perspective, by Avinash Dixit (1996)

The Economic Consequences of Rolling Back the Welfare State, by A. B. Atkinson (1999)

In cooperation with the Council of the Center for Economic Studies of the University of Munich

Martin Beckmann, David F. Bradford, Gebhard Flaig, Otto Gandenberger, Franz Gehrels, Martin Hellwig, Bernd Huber, Mervyn King, John Komlos, Hans Möller, Richard Musgrave, Ray Rees, Bernd Rudolph, Agnar Sandmo, Karlhans Sauernheimer, Hans Schneeweiss, Robert Solow, Wolfgang Wiegard, Charles Wyplosz

The Economic Consequences of Rolling Back the Welfare State

A. B. Atkinson

The MIT Press
Cambridge, Massachusetts
London, England

This book was set in Palatino by Asco Typesetters, Hong Kong.

Printed and bound in the United States of America.

Library of Congress Cataloging-in-Publication Data

Atkinson, A. B. (Anthony Barnes)
    The economic consequences of rolling back the welfare state /
A. B. Atkinson.
        p.   cm. — (Munich lectures in economics)
    Includes bibliographical references and index.
    ISBN 0-262-01171-9 (hc : alk. paper)
    1. Welfare state. 2. Welfare economics. I. Title. II. Series.
HB99.3.A85   1999
330—dc21   99-11116
                                               CIP

Contents

Series Foreword

Every year the CES council awards a prize to an internationally renowned and innovative economist for outstanding contributions to economic research. The scholar is honored with the title "Distinguished CES Fellow" and is invited to give the "Munich Lectures in Economics."

The lectures are held at the Center for Economic Studies of the University of Munich. They introduce areas of recent or potential interest to a wide audience in a nontechnical way and combine theoretical depth with policy relevance.

Hans Werner Sinn
Professor of Economics and Public Finance
Director of CES
University of Munich

Preface

This book contains a revised version of the material presented as the Munich Lectures in Economics at the Centre for Economic Studies, University of Munich, in November 1995. I was very honored by the invitation to give the second set of lectures in this series, following in the footsteps of Avinash Dixit, with whom I shared an office at MIT in my student days.

As Avinash commented, the format of a short book based on three lectures allows the author to set out a larger set of issues than possible in a single article, without requiring full monographic treatment. The subject matter of the present lectures—the economics of the welfare state—is indeed wide ranging, and I could not hope to compress into three hours an adequate review of the many different questions that are raised. I covered only a selection, and this is equally true of the written version. While I have elaborated a number of aspects, there are many important omissions, and the book makes no pretense to give a comprehensive treatment. My aim is to make readers think again about issues they may regard as settled, rather than to give them definitive answers.

The completion of the book has taken longer than I hoped. In part this reflects the excellent comments I have received, which have caused me to rewrite substantial parts. I am most grateful to the following for their constructive and incisive criticism: François Bourguignon, Andrea Brandolini, Avinash Dixit, Bob Goodin, Andrea Ichino, Danièle Meulders, Agnar Sandmo, and Hans-Werner Sinn. Three anonymous reviewers for MIT Press provided detailed and most helpful comments. None of the above is, however, in any way responsible for the remaining errors or for the views expressed. I should thank Judith Atkinson for help in preparing the final manuscript.

Finally, I should like to thank Hans-Werner Sinn and his colleagues in Munich for the warm hospitality I received during my very pleasant visit.

1 The Welfare State under Attack

The welfare state has in recent years come under attack from economists. In many OECD countries there are calls to roll back spending on the welfare state. It is argued that the size of transfer programs is responsible for a decline in economic performance, and that cuts in spending are a prerequisite for a return to the golden age of full employment and economic growth. This applies especially to social transfer expenditure (social security, social assistance, and universal transfers), on which I concentrate here.

The critique of government spending has been especially forceful in Europe, where the welfare state has traditionally played a major role. In Sweden, the Economics Commission, chaired by Assar Lindbeck and including distinguished economists from other Nordic countries, has referred to "the crisis of the Swedish model," arguing that it has "resulted in institutions and structures that today constitute an obstacle to economic efficiency and economic growth because of their lack of flexibility and their one-sided concerns for income safety and distribution, with limited concern for economic incentives" (Lindbeck et al. 1994, p. 17). They seek cuts in social security benefit levels in order that "the social-security (or social insurance) system should not overburden the economy through distorted incentives or large deficits" (Lindbeck et al. 1993, p. 238).

In the European Union, an influential document has been "Growth and Employment: The Scope for a European Initiative," prepared by Jacques Drèze and Edmond Malinvaud, on the basis of discussions with a group of Belgian and French economists. This report emphasizes the positive functions of the welfare state, but lists three major objections:

(i) measures of income protection or social insurance introduce undesired rigidities in the functioning of labour markets;
(ii) welfare programmes increase the size of government at a risk of inefficiency; their funding enhances the amount of revenue to be raised, and so the magnitude of tax distortions;
(iii) welfare programmes may lead to cumulative deficits and mounting public debts. (Drèze and Malinvaud 1994, p. 95)

They conclude that "the agenda should be to make the Welfare State leaner and more efficient" (p. 82). While recognizing the diversity of national circumstances within Europe, and that in some countries spending may be too low, their overall recommendation is to "reduce expenditure in some countries, perhaps by 2 percent of GDP or so" (p. 98).

Powerful voices are calling for a rolling back of the welfare state, and there are undoubtedly objective reasons for a re-examination. The dynamics of the welfare state may be such that it has expanded beyond its optimal scale. Social and economic circumstances have changed since social security programs were first introduced. Population aging on the one hand and adverse labor market shocks on the other have raised the costs of retirement pensions and unemployment benefits. The combination of lower growth rates with higher real rates of interest has reduced the relative attractiveness of state unfunded pension schemes relative to funded pensions.

The proposals to scale back the welfare state have therefore to be treated seriously, but equally we have to examine critically the underlying argument. How exactly does the welfare state represent an obstacle to economic efficiency and economic growth? By what mechanisms is economic performance adversely affected? What can be said on the other side? Are there ways in which the welfare state has a positive role in the modernization of the economy? Is it possible that cuts in state benefits will reduce, rather than increase, the level of employment or the rate of growth?

I should emphasize at the outset that the present book does not attempt to determine whether or not spending should in fact be cut. The reader will find no categorical answer to the question: Should we roll back the welfare state? The aim is rather to clarify the nature of the charges leveled against the welfare state, so that readers can make up their own minds.

1.1 Economists and the Welfare State

What have economists been saying about the welfare state? When I first began studying economics in the early 1960s, few economists were interested in the welfare state. Full employment, rising real wages, state pensions, and child benefit were together assumed to have eliminated poverty. In the United Kingdom, according to *The Times*, there had been a "remarkable improvement—no less than the virtual abolition of the sheerest want" (quoted in Coates and Silburn 1970, p. 14). According to Anthony Crosland (economist, later Foreign Secretary) in *The Future of Socialism*, "primary poverty has been largely eliminated" (1956, p. 59). Social security was a technical topic left to those specializing in social policy, and it was rare for an article on this subject to appear in the *Economic Journal* or *American Economic Review*.

Since then, the pendulum has swung, and the welfare state is now being investigated intensively by economists, as illustrated by the recommendations cited above. Macroeconomists, as well as microeconomists, write about unemployment insurance, invalidity benefit, and the funding of pensions. The welfare state features in a big way in discussions of the budget deficit. Martin Feldstein, whose work has done much to bring about this renewed interest among the economics profession, identified in the 1970s two areas of social security spending that had major adverse effects on economic performance. From his research on retirement pensions and savings, he concluded that "the social security program [in the United States] approximately halves the personal savings rate, [which] implies that it substantially reduces the stock of capital and the level of national income" (1974, p. 922). In his analysis of unemployment insurance, Feldstein concluded that this program encouraged temporary layoffs and that "a reform of unemployment insurance ... could substantially lower the permanent rate of unemployment" (1976b, p. 956). These two programs—retirement pensions and unemployment insurance—will indeed be those to which I pay particular attention in this book.

This rediscovery of the welfare state by economists is much to be welcomed. For many governments social and economic policy are inextricably intertwined. Whatever the Conservative government in the United Kingdom may have thought, the economic development of the European Union cannot be separated from the evolution of its social policy. It makes no sense to discuss economic and social policy in isolation. To a considerable extent, the present problems of the welfare state are the result of economic failures. When advocating austere macroeconomic policies, policymakers often assume that the social costs can be dealt with by a social safety net, but a safety net can easily become overloaded. Conversely, the design of the social transfer system has significant implications for the working of the economy.

Functions of the Welfare State

At the same time, there are several features of the present discussion by economists that I find disturbing. My first reservation is that much of the economic analysis concentrates on the impact of the welfare state on economic performance to the virtual neglect of the functions the welfare state is intended to perform. Cuts in social transfers, for example, are advocated on the grounds that they, or the taxes necessary to finance them, distort the working of the labor market. But any decision about welfare state policy requires us to look at both sides of the balance and at what the welfare state is actually for. The economic costs are relevant, but so too are the benefits in terms of social objectives. Welfare state programs were introduced to meet certain goals, and one has to ask how far these goals could be achieved if a program were cut or eliminated. This is indeed recognized by Feldstein, since in the passage about unemployment insurance from which the quote above was taken he refers to seeking a reform "without reducing the protection that is available to those without work" (1976b, p. 956).

The protection offered by the welfare state is often discussed in terms of the relief of poverty, but this takes too narrow a view of its functions. The reduction of poverty is an important objective, but it is only one of the goals of programs such as retirement pensions, workmens' compensation, invalidity benefit, child benefit, and unemployment insurance. Redistribution is not just a matter of transfers between rich and poor. The welfare state serves to even out differences in life chances, to achieve greater equity between generations, and to redress inequality by race, gender, or health status. More generally, these programs are intended to help people reallocate income over the lifecycle, to insure against events which cause income loss, and to provide a sense of security to all citizens. As Haveman has described it, one important "gain from the welfare state is the universal *reduction in the uncertainty* faced by individuals" (1985).

In this volume I am concentrating on the consequences of the welfare state for the working of the economy—on the cost side of the account—but the success of the welfare state in meeting this plurality of objectives is an important part of the story. (I have discussed this aspect of the balance sheet in Atkinson 1996.)

1.2 Working with, Rather than against, the Grain

My second reservation is that, even concentrating exclusively, as I do here, on the impact of the welfare state on the economy, I believe that the recent economic literature has failed to recognize sufficiently its positive economic functions in a modern industrialized economy. I have already referred to the influential writing of Feldstein to the effect that pay-as-you-go state pensions have lowered the rate of capital accumulation and that unemployment insurance has caused a rise in the so-called natural rate of unemployment. Others have argued that payment of disability benefits causes people to leave the labor force, that retirement pensions cause people to retire early, that social assistance to lone parents discourages labor force participation (see Danziger, Haveman, and Plotnick 1981 for an early and critical review of a number of these dimensions). The calls to roll back the welfare state have been heavily influenced by this highlighting of the disincentive effects.

Some economists have urged a more balanced view. Barr, in his *Journal of Economic Literature* survey, argues that "the welfare state has an efficiency function which is largely separate from its redistributive aims" (1992, p. 742). Sandmo (1991), in his presidential address to the European Economic Association, charted the rise of more critical views about the welfare state but urged caution in swinging too far in that direction. Schmähl has similarly warned, "It would be one-sided and dangerous to view social policy merely ... as something that disturbs the market process.... It is far rather a question of organizing social security in such a way as to minimize losses in efficiency while at the same time making a positive contribution towards that efficiency, so that we avoid being confronted by a 'big trade-off'" (1995, p. 27). The welfare state can work with, rather than against, the grain of economic policy.

The idea that the welfare state may have positive as well as negative efficiency consequences will not come as a totally alien idea to most noneconomists. Historically, social insurance grew up as a complement to the modern employment relationship, guaranteeing workers against catastrophic loss of income through accident, sickness, or unemployment, and hence providing an incentive for people to enter formal employment. In current times, as mature economies transform, it is recognized that people may be more willing to take risks, to retrain, and to change jobs in a society in which there is adequate social protection. As argued by Abramovitz in his presidential address of 1980 to the American Economic Association:

The enlargement of the government's economic role, including its support of income minima, health care, social insurance, and other elements of the welfare state, was ... not just a question of compassionate regard.... It was, and is,—up to a point—a part of the productivity growth process itself. (1981, pp. 2–3)

The emphasis by economists on the negative economic effects of the welfare state can be attributed to the theoretical framework adopted in much policy analysis, which remains rooted in a model of perfectly competitive and perfectly clearing markets. In this first-best situation, any real-world tax or transfer necessarily causes a loss of efficiency. Put another way, the theoretical framework incorporates none of the contingencies for which the welfare state exists. There is no uninsured uncertainty in the model, nor involuntary unemployment, nor is the future introduced in any meaningful way. The whole purpose of welfare state provision is missing from the theoretical model.

Recognition that the real-world economy departs from the competitive equilibrium model does not necessarily imply that the welfare state takes on a benign role from the standpoint of efficiency. It is conceivable that state intervention reinforces, rather than corrects, departures from full employment. Unemployment insurance may make it more attractive for workers to queue for union jobs, increasing the "natural rate" of unemployment.[1] But this is not true of all departures from the competitive equilibrium model. Other starting points reflecting advances in economic theory, such as those on imperfect information stressed by Barr (1992), provide a different perspective. Unemployment insurance may, for instance, have the effect of increasing the level of employment in "good jobs." As I shall argue in this book, the welfare state may have a wide variety of consequences, some positive and some negative, as far as the working of the economy is concerned.

Although it is not the focus of this book, the same is true of adopting a macroeconomic perspective. Interestingly, fifty years ago the economics of the welfare state was discussed much more from the standpoint of macroeconomics. In the preface to *The Economics of Social Security*, published in 1941,

Harris refers to the influence of Keynes, to whom his book is dedicated, and the "need for a study of social security that would utilize the recent developments in theory and especially in the fields of money, fiscal policy, and economic fluctuations" (p. vii). Peacock, in *The Economics of National Insurance*, says:

At the present stage of evolution of national insurance, it is probably true to say that the traditional economic problems of this form of social security, e.g. the relationship between wage rates and insurance, the particular incidence of social security taxation, insurance as a deterrent of labour mobility, etc., are of less interest and importance than the relationship between it and general economic policy as directed by the State. (1952, p. 51)

From the standpoint of demand management, social transfers—particularly unemployment insurance—were seen as contributing to the degree of automatic stabilization. The development of the welfare state was complementary with concerns for full employment. When Lord Beveridge prepared his proposals for *Full Employment in a Free Society* (1944), he did not see them as conflicting with his plan for the postwar welfare state, *Social Insurance and Allied Services* (1942). It is, I believe, no coincidence that when the welfare state was viewed from a macroeconomic perspective, its economic impact was regarded by economists in a more positive light.

1.3 Importance of Institutional Features

My third reservation is that the analysis by economists of the welfare state tends to ignore its institutional structure. While all modeling must abstract from the details of social security provision, which can be arcane in the extreme, we must be sure that the abstraction does not neglect important economic features. In the case of social security this appears often to be the case, and key elements of the law and its administration are missing.

Unemployment benefit provides an illustration of the neglect of important institutional structure. Economic models regularly assume that the only relevant condition for the receipt of benefit is being unemployed. In fact, in the typical unemployment insurance program, benefit is subject to contribution conditions, is paid for a limited duration, and is monitored to check that the person is making genuine efforts to seek employment. Benefit may be refused where the person entered unemployment voluntarily or as a result of industrial misconduct, and a person may be disqualified for refusing job offers.

The conditions for the receipt of unemployment insurance not only reduce its coverage but also affect the relationship between transfers and the working of the economy. The standard job search model, for example, assumes that workers can reject job offers that offer less than a specified wage. Such a reservation wage strategy may, however, lead to the person being disqualified from benefit. This institutional feature needs to be incorporated and may change the predicted impact. A second example is provided by the general equilibrium formulation of the job search model by Albrecht and Axell (1984). This makes a most valuable contribution by endogenizing the wage offer distribution, but the assumptions made about the operation of unemployment benefit ignore its institutional structure. In the model of Albrecht and Axell, the unemployed consist entirely of those who have not held a job, which means that they cannot satisfy the usual contribution conditions attached to unemployment insurance. (In addition, they have rejected a low wage job offer, for which they would risk being disqualified.) A third example is provided by a different labor market model: the shirking version of the efficiency wage hypothesis advanced by Shapiro and Stiglitz (1984), among others. Worker effort depends on the risk of being fired, and the cost of being fired is assumed to be that the worker has to live on unemployment benefit. But dismissal for shirking is likely to lead to disqualification from benefit. Employers have a strong incentive to report job loss as resulting from misconduct, insofar as there are statutory redundancy payments, because this would reduce employer liability.

Unemployment benefit has been taken as an illustration, since it is one of the programs on which I concentrate in the following chapters, but in other areas of social policy, too, there is a tendency for economists to analyze the impact of a hypothetical benefit that differs in essential features from real-world social security.

1.4 Political Economy

My fourth, and final, reservation concerns the public choice aspects of the welfare state. Here research by economists has contributed substantially to our understanding of the political factors underlying the evolution of the welfare state. Sandmo refers to

the gap between the potential for welfare improvements through public policy and the actual progress made through the policy process.... [P]art of the reason for this gap must be sought in the private incentive mechanisms within which the politicians and bureaucrats operate. Although I believe that this insight has been present ... for a considerable time, the public choice school has made a valuable contribution in offering a more general perspective on the relationship between politics and economics. (1991, p. 236)

Becker (1985), Lindbeck (1985) and Kristov, Lindert, and McClelland (1992), for example, have examined the role of pressure and interest groups in securing expansion of social

spending programs. There have been models of income redistribution governed by majority voting (such as Perotti 1993).
Lindbeck (1995b) has emphasised the role of endogenous
habits and social norms. He draws attention to the possibility of multiple equilibria and argues that "the hazardous
dynamics" mean "the welfare state will destroy its own economic foundations" (1995a, p. 9). Saint-Paul (1994, 1995) has
pointed to the existence of "politico-economic complemen-
tarities," by which "a poor labour market is associated with
support for a poor policy" (1995, p. 575).

These public choice analyses are important, and they draw
on a long tradition of fiscal sociology (see, for example, Musgrave 1986). However, there are two aspects that give me
cause for concern. The first is that there is as yet no general
agreement on models of political behavior. While the utility-
maximizing model of individual consumption and labor supply
decisions is open to a number of important objections, it nev-
ertheless enjoys among economists a degree of agreement that
does not apply to models of political behavior. As Musgrave
has argued, the "process reflects the interaction of pluralistic
interests and interest groups. This plurality renders fiscal deci-
sion-making complex and difficult to predict, which is unfortu-
nate; but it is hardly reason for adopting an over-simplified
model that gives ready but frequently mistaken answers"
(1986, p. 184). His criticism is directed at class-based theories,
but the same objection applies to the median voter model,
which has received a great deal of attention from economists. I
do not feel that we can be confident in assigning pride of place
to the median voter, political ideology, or bureaucratic latitude. Even if we felt happy adopting a median voter explanation, there are a wide range of considerations. Voters may or
may not act according to their own interests; their conception
of their interests may encompass concern for others. If that is a

valid criticism of models of political behavior, then we need to examine the sensitivity of the conclusions to the choice of model. Before concluding that the growth of spending is the result of political pressure, or that there are hazardous dynamics to the welfare state, we must see how far the findings depend on the assumptions made about voter preferences or alternative models. There has been relatively little research that has set side by side different possible explanations of the development of social security and examined the sensitivity of the conclusions to the choice of model.

The other ground for concern is that the discussion of the economic impact of the welfare state appears to pay little attention to the context in which it has become a subject of public debate. Why are we discussing the retrenchment of the welfare state? In part because, as outlined earlier, it is believed that the welfare state has itself had an adverse effect on the economy. But it is also, in part, on account of the exogenous shocks experienced by the economy. These include productivity shocks and demographic shocks. We have to see the proposals to roll back the welfare state as a reaction to this type of disturbance.

The upsurge in public debate may also owe something to the writing of economists, such as those cited earlier, highlighting the adverse consequences of social transfers. It has long seemed to me ironic that economists so concerned with the endogeneity of policy decisions appear not be aware of their own role in the process. The evolution of the welfare state over the past century has undoubtedly been influenced by the thinking of social scientists. What economists are writing today similarly affects the way in which politicians and voters conceive of the welfare state. We have to consider the role of economists themselves in the political process. To this the present book is no exception, but I have tried to make explicit in this introduction the way I feel the debate should be shifted.

1.5   Structure of the Book

The principal concern of this book is the theoretical analysis of the welfare state, but before turning to theory I examine empirical evidence, which often is the main ingredient in the public debate. In chapter 2 I consider the aggregate empirical evidence about welfare state spending as a proportion of gross domestic product (GDP), which appears to underlie much of the case against the welfare state. Countries with high spending, it is alleged, have a poorer economic performance. However, not only is the evidence mixed, but also such an argument is more difficult to establish than it may at first appear: the chapter describes a number of the problems with aggregate cross-country evidence. These include the dynamic specification (does a large welfare state reduce the *level* of output or its *rate of growth*?), problems in measuring the size of the welfare state, and the need to look at the fine structure ($x\%$ of GDP may be spent in very different ways). In particular, the interpretation of such studies depends on the underlying theoretical framework, and this provides the main motivation for the rest of these lectures.

Much discussion of the economic impact of the welfare state appears to be based on a relatively simple model of the functioning of the economy: the microeconomic textbook model of competitive equilibrium. In such a context, scaling back social transfers and the taxes necessary to finance them has the effect of raising employment and output. As I have already indicated, I feel this choice of point of departure unduly influences the conclusions drawn, but it provides a benchmark from which to judge the consequences of alternative approaches. I therefore start chapter 3 with a version of this model. This allows us to identify a number of issues relevant to determining the impact of cutting back on social security benefits and taxes. Are we concerned with the possibility that the welfare state reduces output, or with the possible distortion of economic decisions? These are two different criteria that are often confused. Is it the tax cost of social transfers that matters, or do the transfers themselves have adverse economic impact? (If a Martian offered to fund the unemployment insurance scheme, should we refuse?) If the welfare state is rolled back, what would take its place?

The consequences of departing from the simple competitive equilibrium model depend very much on the way in which economic behavior is formulated. The second half of chapter 3, and chapter 4, are concerned with introducing unemployment. There are many possible explanations of unemployment. In chapter 3 I look at a model where market employment is subject to the risk of involuntary termination, where job matching takes time, and wages are determined by collective bargaining between trade unions and employers. Payment of unemployment benefit in such a context encourages people to queue for union jobs, and scaling back benefits reduces the length of the unemployment queue. This model may characterize the position of those who see unions and unemployment pay as combining to cause European unemployment. At the same time, the scaling back may also lead to a reduction of employment to the extent that the wage has to rise to offset the fall in the "social wage."

Chapter 3 treats unemployment benefit in the same way as most economics textbooks, as simply a wage paid by the state when a person is not working. However, as already noted, this ignores important institutional features of real-world unemployment programs, features that may mitigate the disincentive effect of benefits. Chapter 4 begins by setting out the key institutional characteristics of unemployment benefits. It then sets out a different model of the labor market, allowing for unequal market opportunities. There is labor market segmentation, with a primary sector offering "good jobs" and a secondary sector offering "bad jobs." In the primary sector wages are determined by collective bargaining (as in the model of chapter 3) and workers require no monitoring. Relations with workers are different in the secondary sector; they are not monitored directly but are induced to supply effort by the payment of an efficiency wage premium. In this case, cutting back benefit levels or coverage may affect both the efficiency wage premium and the union differential. Whether scaling back the welfare state increases or reduces employment depends on a number of factors, including the institutional features of the transfer system, different flows in the labor market, and the relative insecurity of jobs in the two sectors.

Cutting back of unemployment benefit is a policy that has been pursued strongly in the United Kingdom, but other countries have followed different policies. The reasons why governments have reacted in different ways to labor market shocks is the subject of chapter 5, which is a case study in the political economy of social security. Different public choice explanations are considered for the reductions in benefit levels and coverage, and I show how, even adopting a straightforward median voter model, one can arrive at different interpretations of the pressure to cut back the welfare state. These different interpretations take on special significance when we allow for the different types of labor market shock that have been observed. We need to consider alternatives to the median voter explanation, including principal/agency relationships, political slack, and the operation of pressure groups.

The theoretical models of chapters 3 and 4 are concerned with the impact of social security on the level of output; in chapter 6 we turn to the effect on the rate of growth, now taking retirement pensions as the main example. It is often contended that the existence of a pay-as-you-go state pension scheme reduces the level of private savings, and that, if the government makes no offsetting adjustment to public savings, this reduces the rate of growth. Chapter 6 examines this argument, drawing on the theory of economic growth. What happens if there is a reduction in the state pension? Does this cause the economy to grow faster? How does the answer depend on what is put in place of the state pension?

The new growth theory concentrates largely on the role of savings. It is supposed that changes in savings are automatically translated into changes in investment without specification of the underlying mechanism. Chapter 7 considers the nature of the investment function, drawing on the theory of the growth of the corporate enterprise. The theory gives prominence to the function of the capital market in influencing the stock market value of firms and hence their investment decisions. The rolling back of state unfunded pensions, and their replacement by private funded pensions, has implications for the capital market, which may operate in the opposite direction from the positive impact on savings.

The final chapter, chapter 8, draws together the main conclusions. These conclusions concern the impact of the welfare state on economic performance. As already explained, I do not here consider the success of social transfers in meeting the objectives they are intended to perform, such as the alleviation of poverty, the redistribution of income across the life cycle, and the provision of a sense of security. For this reason, the book does not provide an overall balance sheet.

1.6 Limitations

The economics of the welfare state is a big subject, and I make
no claim to have covered more than a few aspects. There are
many ways in which social transfers may affect, negatively or
positively, the working of a modern economy. I have not discussed, for example, the impact of social transfers on human
capital formation and the financing of education. The welfare
state may help people afford to stay on at school, or the taxes
necessary to finance it may act as a disincentive to acquiring
qualifications. I have not considered the way in which social
security may affect the willingness of people to take risks, and
the role of the welfare state in providing insurance. It should
be reiterated that I concentrate on cash transfers (social security and social assistance) and do not consider other elements
of the welfare state such as spending on state education or
health care, or related measures such as active labor market
programs. In view of the direct role these elements may play
in human capital formation, it may be seen that I am inten-
tionally tackling the areas where the efficiency critique of the
welfare state seems most likely to apply. Moreover, within the
field of cash transfers, as signaled earlier, I concentrate on unemployment benefits and retirement pensions, saying nothing
about health insurance, injury or disability benefits, nor insurance for long-term care. The book focuses on only two of the
pillars of the welfare state, albeit two that are central to its
construction.

   One of the purposes of the lectures is to demonstrate the
relevance of economic principles in understanding a range of
welfare state issues. A general equilibrium approach is necessary to consider the implications of social transfers for wage
levels and wage differentials (chapters 3 and 4) and for interest
and profit rates (chapters 6 and 7). Principal-agent relation-

ships are important in the efficiency wage theory of chapter 4, in the political economy analysis of chapter 5, and in the shareholder-management separation of chapter 7. Interest groups appear in the form of trade unions in chapters 3 and 4, pressure groups in chapter 5, and pension providers in chapter 7. At the same time, the range of economic theories on which I draw means that I cannot do justice to any of them. I am using the theory of the firm, consumer theory, growth theory, and elements of modern macroeconomics, but leave many of their subtleties undiscussed.

A further important omission is that I consider a single country in isolation. The economic models are those of countries closed to international trade and factor movements. Yet some of the most pressing issues concerning the welfare state are those arising from international competition and fiscal competition within economic unions. The welfare state may be under threat if labor and capital move in response to differential financing costs, or political pressure may achieve the same outcome. These issues are discussed by, among others, Sinn (1990) and Atkinson (1992b).

The institutional context, on which I have laid great stress, is itself a limitation. The fact that differences in institutions lead to differences in economic outcomes means that one cannot claim generality for one's findings. The features discussed in this book are broadly those of Western European countries, but are not necessarily directly applicable to any one country. Historically, the welfare state has developed in different ways in different European countries. The Nordic tradition is not the same as that in, say, Germany, and the German system in turn does not look like that in the United Kingdom. Programs with similar names perform different functions in different countries. It is for this reason misleading to talk about "*the* European welfare state"; and the policy reform appropriate to one country may be irrelevant, or damaging, in another. As put to me by one reader of the draft version of these lectures, "a critical attitude to the Swedish welfare state does not imply that the British welfare state be rolled back."

The diversity of European Union countries is well illustrated by the projections of public pension expenditure published in *European Economy* (Franco and Munzi 1996), showing projected state spending on pensions as a proportion of GDP. We know that this figure is predicted to be high in Germany— around 17.5 percent in the year 2030—and in the Netherlands and France, but this is not true in all countries, notably in the United Kingdom, where the figure is little more than 5 percent. (In all cases I have taken the best case scenarios.) This makes a great deal of difference when considering the future. People who call for a reduction in spending on the welfare state of 1 or 2 percent of GDP, with pensions being a principal target, must recognize that such a reduction would have very different implications in different member states.

There was once a famous, probably apocryphal, English newspaper headline, "Fog in Channel: Continent Isolated," and no doubt I have been unduly influenced by what has happened in the United Kingdom. At the same time, the United Kingdom has perhaps advanced furthest of European countries in the direction of rolling back the welfare state, so that our experience may be of interest to those on the mainland.

2 Welfare State and Economic Performance: Aggregate Empirical Evidence

Does a large welfare state depress economic performance? Does it cause output to fall below potential or for the annual growth rate to be lower than in countries without such a level of transfers? In seeking answers it is tempting to look at measures of the size of spending on the welfare state, typically expressed as a proportion of gross domestic product (GDP), as in the OECD statistics for social security transfers (1997, Table 6.3). This is a common procedure in empirical studies, and it is my starting point here.

Some countries are well known to have relatively small welfare states. Figure 2.1 shows the OECD figures for the ratio to GDP of spending on social security transfers in 1995.[2] For the United States, the ratio was around 13 percent, which is considerably below the average for the European Union, which was 20 percent. The United States figure is virtually the same as that in Japan, and not very different from that in the United Kingdom, which was 15 percent (in 1994), but it is around half that in the Netherlands. Expenditure in Germany is about two percentage points below the European Union average, that in Sweden about three percentage points higher.

The relative positions of different countries have not always been the same. In some countries social transfers have

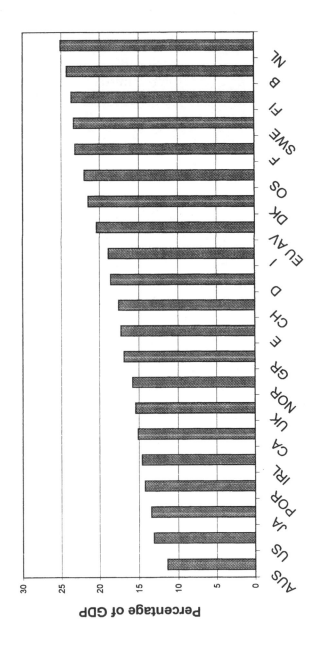

Figure 2.1
Social security transfers in OECD countries, 1995. Source: OECD 1995, table 6.3. The figures for Ireland and the United Kingdom relate to 1994; the figure for Portugal relates to 1993.

increased faster over time as a percentage of GDP than in others, as is shown for a selection of countries in figure 2.2. In 1960 West Germany had spending about half as large again as Sweden, but it was overtaken by Sweden around 1978, and the latter has now risen above France. It may also be noted that in the 1980s the United States and the United Kingdom both had governments pledged to rolling back the frontier of the state, but that spending at the end of the decade was much the same as at the beginning. The evidence on spending trends in figure 2.2 bears out the claim for the United Kingdom by Le Grand that "welfare policy successfully weathered ... an ideological blizzard in the 1980s" (1990, p. 350). Aggregate figures may, however, be misleading for reasons that are explored below.[3]

In this chapter, we see what can be learned by looking at the relation between aggregate social security spending and economic performance, seeking to identify different hypotheses and bring out the problems of interpretation.

2.1 Different Hypotheses

The availability of such aggregate data on a comparable basis for different countries means that it is tempting to see how far there is an association with differences in economic performance. A European Commission (1993) report, for example, has plotted social expenditure against the level of GDP per head. A version of this diagram, using the OECD social security transfer data described above, is shown in figure 2.3, where GDP per head is compared across countries using exchange parities that allow for differences in purchasing power. Although there is quite a lot of variation among countries with similar GDP per head (for example, between Italy and the Netherlands), there is clearly, within Europe, a tendency for

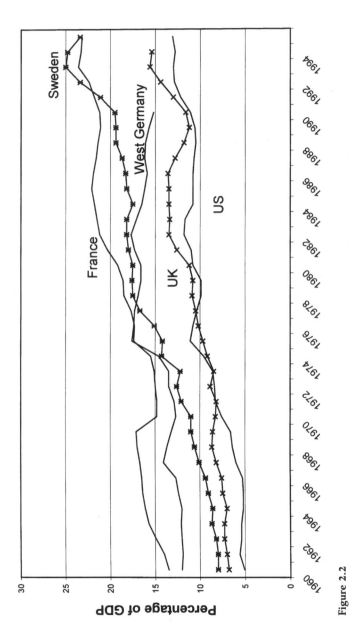

Figure 2.2
Growth of social security transfers, 1960–1995. Source: OECD 1995, table 6.3 (full set of data available on Statwise diskette). The figures for West Germany end in 1990.

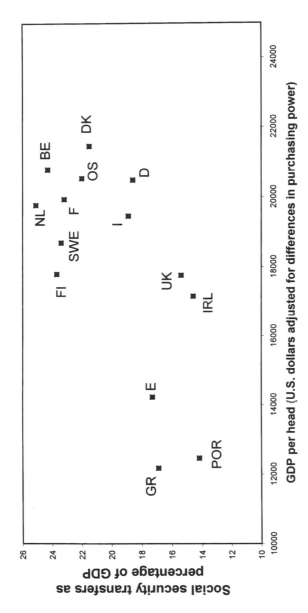

Figure 2.3
Social security transfers and GDP per head, 1995. Source: OECD 1995, tables C and 6.3. The social security figures for Ireland and the United Kingdom relate to 1994; the figure for Portugal relates to 1993.

the richer countries to have the largest welfare states. The countries with relatively low spending included, at that time, Greece, Ireland, and Portugal.

From this we draw at once one obvious lesson: a statistical correlation between economic performance indicators and the size of the welfare state cannot necessarily be ascribed to an underlying causal mechanism. One manifestly cannot argue directly from the observed relation that higher welfare spending leads to higher national income. While this is one hypothesis, the causation could well run the other way. It may be that it is successful countries, with high income per head, that can afford a more generous social security system. There is indeed a long history of studies in both political science and economics seeking to explain cross-country differences in the ratio of transfer spending to GDP by the level of national income and other variables, such as the existence of governments of different political complexions and the age of the social security system. Not all of these studies have found a significant relationship with GDP (for example, Aaron (1967) concluded that, at that time, a higher level of GDP was associated with a lower level of social security spending). Wilensky (1975) found that "[o]ver the long pull, economic level is the root cause of welfare-state development, but its effects are felt chiefly through demographic changes of the past century and the momentum of the programs themselves, once established" (p. 47). This direction of possible causality continues to be taken seriously; for example, a chapter in the recent *New Handbook of Political Science* (Hofferbert and Cingranelli 1996, p. 600) takes as an illustration of the comparative method an equation explaining unemployment insurance by the level of economic development (and the presence of social democratic governments).

Alternatively, there could be no causal relation between GNP and welfare state spending. Both variables may be associated with a third mechanism. We could hypothesize that industrialization of the economy leads both to higher living standards and to the need for social security. Employment in industry, with its risk of catastrophic income loss, creates the role for social insurance; increasing occupational specialization increases income risk. We might therefore expect France or Germany to have larger welfare states than countries like Greece or Portugal, which have a higher proportion of the population in traditional or informal sectors.

A second lesson that emerges at this juncture is the need to distinguish between two different versions of the causal hypothesis. The first is that there is a relation between the size of the welfare state and the level of GDP. This kind of association is referred to below as a *Levels Hypothesis*. Alternatively, there could be a relation between the size of the welfare State and the rate of growth of GDP. This kind of relationship is referred to as a *Growth Rate Hypothesis*. The distinction between these two hypotheses is illustrated in figure 2.4. Suppose there are two countries, A and B, identical in all relevant respects until the date marked with an arrow. At that date, spending on the welfare state is changed in country A in such a direction as to have beneficial consequences for GDP. In the case of the Levels Hypothesis, shown by path 1, we would expect country A to grow faster initially, but to tend to a higher level of GDP. In the long run it grows at the same rate as country B. In contrast, with the Growth Rate Hypothesis GDP grows permanently at a higher rate in country A than in country B (see path 2 in figure 2.4). In the latter case, the paths of GDP would steadily diverge, a prospect that seems to generate much of the anxiety expressed in public debate. People seem to have a particular fear of falling progressively further and further behind their neighbors.

In reality it may be difficult to distinguish between the early years of the two paths shown in figure 2.4. We may not know

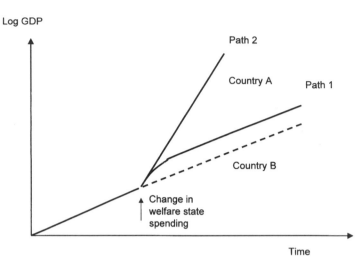

Figure 2.4
Levels Hypothesis and Growth Rate Hypothesis

whether the higher growth rate in country A will be sustained. Nonetheless, the distinction is an important one in principle since it points to rather different kinds of economic models. The levels hypothesis has typically been framed in terms of the relation between output and employment, the arguement being that the welfare state leads to higher unemployment or nonparticipation in the labor force. Here we are in the territory of the macroeconomics of the labor market. In most macro-economic textbooks this is to be found in a different chapter from the growth theory that underlies the growth rate version of the hypothesis. It is with the latter that I begin here.

2.2 Econometric Studies of Aggregate Growth Rates

Can the level of social transfers, expressed as a proportion of GDP, explain part of the differences in growth rates? In 1980 the ratio of spending to GDP in the Netherlands was 15 percentage points higher than in the United States (OECD 1992, table 6.3). What would have happened if the Netherlands had cut its spending by $7\frac{1}{2}$ percentage points and the United States had increased its spending by the same amount? How would growth rates have differed since 1980? Would the United States have been handicapped?

For some people it is self-evident that the scale of social transfers is an important determinant of the trend rate of growth. Other people do not even include this variable in extensive lists of explanatory variables. For instance, Barro in his cross-country empirical studies (1997; Barro and Sala-i-Martin 1995) finds that government consumption lowers the growth rate, but does not look at social transfer expenditure. The OECD review of the determinants of productivity performance (Englander and Gurney 1994) does not highlight the welfare state. Nor can one extrapolate from studies that look at total government expenditure, since the impact of different types of government spending may be quite different. For instance, Smith (1975) found that the growth rate of real GDP per capita in the period 1961–1972 was negatively related to public spending excluding transfers, but that the effect was smaller and less significant when public spending included transfers. He argues that "it is less economically harmful for the state to raise taxes and make transfer payments than to consume resources directly" (p. 29). Without necessarily accepting that all resource use is harmful for economic growth (for example, research outlays may contribute to raising growth rates), we clearly need to look at transfer spending on its own. What is more, we have to distinguish between different types of transfer. Payment of debt interest, for example, appears to be a separate category that needs to be excluded when considering the impact of social transfers. Similarly, we want to distinguish between transfers to households and transfers to companies. Grants to a company to encourage it to open a factory in Wales cannot be expected to have an identical economic impact to that of unemployment benefit paid to ex-miners in Wales.

It is also evident that in considering how far countries with large welfare states have grown more slowly, we must control for other influences on economic performance. Wall (1995) has shown that in a regression of growth rates on dummy variables as to whether countries play baseball or cricket, baseball playing countries have significantly higher rates of growth. Although he says that the empirical results speak for themselves, I suspect that they do so with their tongues firmly in their cheeks. In order to learn about the impact of the welfare state, or of sport, we have to embed the statistical analysis within a model of the determinants of growth, as in the work on growth empirics by Barro (1991) and Mankiw, Romer, and Weil (1992).

A central model used in the literature on growth is that based on an aggregate production function, where aggregate output (GDP), Y, is a function of capital, K, and labor, L. In the literature on the sources of growth (Solow 1957; Denison 1962, 1967), it is common to decompose the growth rate into the separate contributions of capital and labor, with the residual being attributed to productivity growth. This can be done straightforwardly in the case of the Cobb-Douglas version of the production function with constant returns to capital and labor:

$$Y = AK^{\beta}L^{1-\beta}, \tag{2.1}$$

where A denotes the level of productivity, so that technical progress is reflected in the growth of A. This functional form is used below, but it should be remembered that it is a special form. As is well known, it has the property that the competitive share of profits in the value of output is constant, equal to β, with the competitive share of labor equal to $(1 - \beta)$. We may write in the Cobb-Douglas case:

Growth rate of GDP

$$= \beta \times \text{Growth rate of capital}$$

$$+ (1 - \beta) \times \text{Growth rate of labor}$$

$$+ \text{Rate of technical progress.} \qquad (2.2)$$

The logic of this decomposition has been questioned by a number of authors, who see these elements as interdependent: the rate of productivity growth depending on the rate of investment. I return to this argument in chapter 6 when discussing new growth theory. If, however, the decomposition (2.2) is valid, then we can identify separate channels by which the welfare state may influence the rate of growth. Social transfers might affect either the growth of factor supply (capital and labor) or the growth of productivity, or of course both. The payment of pay-as-you-go state pensions, for instance, may reduce capital formation, and hence the growth of output by an amount which depends on β. Alternatively, the existence of a social safety net may encourage the risk-taking necessary to engage in the inventive activity that leads to new ideas and new techniques of production. This would show up in the rate of technical progress, that is, in the growth of factor productivity.

There have been a number of empirical studies of aggregate growth examining in this way the role of social transfers, and ten such studies are brought together in the appendix.[4] The main features are summarized in table 2.1. The table shows that part of the findings of these studies that relates to transfer

Table 2.1
Summary of studies of growth rates and social transfers

Study	Coverage	Period	Countries	Results: effect of 5 percentage point reduction in WS
Landau 1985	Pooled time series/ cross-section	Annual growth rates 1952–76	16 OECD inc. Japan	NOT SIGNIFICANT
Korpi 1985	Mixed time series/ cross-section	Period 1950–73 and subperiods	17 OECD exc. Japan	*0.9 percentage point reduction in annual growth rate*
Weede 1986	Pooled time series/ cross-section	1960–82 subperiods	19 OECD inc. Japan	1 percentage point increase in annual growth rate
McCallum and Blais 1987	Pooled time series/ cross-section	1960–83 subperiods	17 OECD inc. Japan	*0.5 percentage point reduction in annual growth rate*
Castles and Dowrick 1990	Pooled time series/ cross-section	1960–85 subperiods	18 OECD inc. or exc. Japan	*0.3–4 percentage point reduction in annual growth rate*
Weede 1991	Pooled time series/ cross-section	1960–85 subperiods	19 OECD inc. Japan	0.5 percentage point increase in annual growth rate

Sala-i-Martin 1992	Cross-country	1970–85	74 world-wide	*0.6 percentage point reduction in annual growth rate*
Nordström 1992	Cross-country	1977–89	14 OECD inc. or exc. Japan	0.6 percentage point increase in annual growth rate
Hansson and Henrekson 1994	Cross-country/ cross-industry	1970–87	14 OECD inc. Japan	NOT SIGNIFICANT
Persson and Tabellini 1994	Cross-country	1960–85	13 OECD inc. Japan	0.3 percentage point increase in annual growth rate

payments; it should be stressed that the authors cited are not concerned solely with the impact of social transfers, and that in some cases it represents only a minor part of their results. To give a flavor of the approach adopted, we may take the study by Castles and Dowrick (1990), which was explicitly concerned with the impact of government spending. They estimated a set of regression equations based on equation 2.2, with the addition of the following variables: initial per capita GDP (catch-up variable), index of institutional sclerosis, and government expenditure variables. The same variables, and population growth, are assumed to enter the determination of the growth rate of capital and employment, and hence allow us to compare the effect of welfare state spending on factor productivity with that on the total growth rate.

The results of this kind of aggregate analysis are mixed, as may be seen by looking at the last column in table 2.1, which shows the predicted impact of a reduction in welfare state spending equal to 5 percentage points of GDP (approximately the difference between Austria and Greece). The studies are classified into three groups: those that find no significant relation between welfare state spending and the rate of growth (shown in capitals), those that find a significant negative relation (shown in ordinary type), and those that find a positive relation (shown in italics). Of the ten studies, two (Landau 1985 and Hansson and Henrekson 1994) find an insignificant effect of the transfer variable on annual growth rates, four (Weede 1986; Weede 1991; Nordström 1992; and Persson and Tabellini 1994) find that transfers are negatively associated with average growth, and four (Korpi 1985; Castles and Dowrick 1990; McCallum and Blais 1987; and Sala-i-Martin 1992) find a positive sign to the coefficient of the transfer variable. According to Weede, "social security transfers reduce growth rates rather strongly" (1986, p. 506), whereas, according to

Korpi, "social security expenditures ... show positive and significant relationships with economic growth" (1985, p. 108).

2.3   Assessing the Findings about Growth Rates

Simple "vote counting" among different studies is a potentially misleading way of summarizing the findings (Hedges and Olkin 1985, chapter 4), and a more systematic approach is desirable. Several readers of the first draft of these lectures have indeed asked why I have not applied meta-analysis (formal methods for combining evidence across studies). The situation is, however, different from that where meta-analysis is applied in fields such as education or social psychology, where different studies use different samples of, say, college students. Here, there are some issues related to the selection of data: for example, sensitivity in some, but not all, cases to the country coverage, notably the inclusion or exclusion of Japan (see table 2.1). There are also differences in the time period covered or the subperiods selected. But, in a broad sense, the same macroeconomic data underlie the studies reviewed here, and the issue is largely one of model specification, not of different datasets.

Several authors have sought to reconcile the differences in findings that arise from different specifications, including Saunders (1986), McCallum and Blais (1987), Castles and Dowrick (1990), and Weede (1991).[5] Even if they do not adopt a formal approach to model selection, these authors have added to our understanding by comparing their results with those of earlier studies and seeking to explain the differences in findings.[6] Among the explanations that have been advanced are:

1. differences between studies seeking to explain the total growth rate (total effect), and those explaining the growth of factor productivity,

2. differences of view as to whether it is appropriate to include dummy variables shifting the intercept for different subperiods,

3. different definitions of the social transfer variable, in particular the inclusion in some cases of other government transfers apart from social security; as already noted, one would expect the impact of subsidies to firms to be rather different,[7]

4. different right-hand variables apart from social transfers, such as the "institutional sclerosis" variable included by Castles and Dowrick (1990).

The appendix table differentiates between studies seeking to explain the total growth rate and those explaining the growth of factor productivity as in the model (2.2), controling for the contribution of factor input growth (investment and employment). Castles and Dowrick (1990) find different results for the total growth rate and for factor productivity. Social transfers, on this basis, have a positive effect on productivity but a negative impact on factor supply, leaving the total growth rate unchanged. This pattern is not, however, consistent with the results of other studies of the total effect that find either a positive or a negative effect on the total growth rate. Nor is it consistent with those studies that have found a negative or insignificant effect on productivity, such as Landau (1985) and Hansson and Henrekson (1994).

The studies listed in table 2.1 have used a variety of methods to overcome the problem of establishing the direction of causality. Some use the initial period value of the social transfer variable on the grounds that regressions of growth rates of GDP on initial levels of the transfer variable would not be subject to simultaneity. This, however, raises an issue concerning the dynamic specification of the estimated relationship. Suppose there is a negative relationship between social

transfers and the level of GDP. In an econometric equation with GDP as the left-hand variable, we might want to include both current and lagged values of the transfer variable in order to allow for delayed responses to changes. For instance, if higher pensions were to reduce aggregate savings, then the capital stock, and hence output, would fall gradually to its new long-run level. But what long-run restrictions do we want to impose on the estimated relationship? As has been stressed in time series econometrics, it is here that economic theory has an important role to play.

There are indeed two different theoretical predictions, as we have seen earlier. The first is that described above as the Levels Hypothesis, where GDP depends on the size of the welfare state. A cut in social spending induces a temporary rise in the growth rate as GDP rises to its new equilibrium level, but there is no permanent increase in the rate of growth. Cast in growth rate terms, the growth rate is related to the change in the level of spending.[8] The alternative theoretical model is that where the level of transfers affects the long-run rate of growth, referred to above as the Growth Rate Hypothesis. In this case, a cut in the welfare state is predicted to raise the growth rate permanently. An explicit distinction between these two hypotheses and the restrictions on coefficients that they imply might help sort out the differences in the empirical studies.

The next generation of aggregate empirical studies will no doubt build on earlier work, and a systematic exploration of the different dimensions should reduce the degree of variety in the results. Not all specifications are equally appropriate, and more sophisticated econometric procedures may lead to results that exhibit greater robustness. At the same time, I must confess to doubts whether effects of the size estimated to date are really plausible. Suppose we go back to the counter-

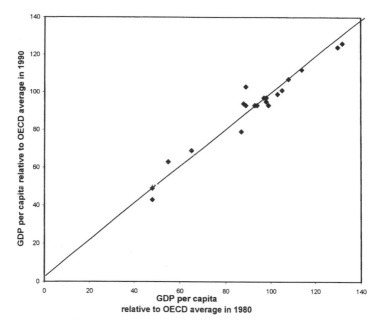

Figure 2.5
GDP per head of OECD countries (adjusted for purchasing power differences) in 1990 compared with 1980. Source: OECD 1994b, p. 145. Iceland, Luxembourg, and Turkey are not included.

factual question posed at the outset of the previous section. In 1980 the ratio of spending to GDP in the Netherlands was 15 percentage points higher than in the United States. What would have happened if the Netherlands had cut its spending by $7\frac{1}{2}$ percentage points and the U.S. had increased its spending by the same amount? How would economic performance have been different?

To see this, I have plotted in figure 2.5 the relationship between relative GDP per head (measured in terms of purchasing power) in different OECD countries in 1990 compared with 1980. In each case the GDP per head is expressed relative to

the average, so that a country at 100 in both years is at the average in both. Some countries, like Spain, Finland, and Luxembourg, lie above the 45° line, indicating that they have grown faster than the average; others, like the Netherlands and Switzerland, lie below. But, overall, countries tended to grow over the decade at broadly the same rate. Most are close to the 45° line.

I now consider what would have happened if Netherlands and the United States had changed their policy in the way described, using two of the estimated relationships: that of Weede (1986) and that of Korpi (1985). The first of these studies finds that the welfare State has a large negative effect on growth, so that elimination of the differences means that countries with large welfare states, like the Netherlands, are predicted to perform better without this handicap. The reverse is true of the United States. The findings for these two countries are shown in figure 2.6 by the squares marked NL- and US-, respectively. What is striking is the quantitative magnitude: Netherlands would, on this set of estimates, have nearly caught up the U.S. in a decade. I do not find this entirely believable. Nor do I find the reverse believable. In figure 2.6 the point NL+ (US+ is off the graph) shows what would have happened if larger social transfers improved growth, as in the estimates of Korpi (1985), so that a leveling up of spending in the United States now means that it performs better. Conversely, the Netherlands, without the predicted boost it gets to its growth rate from its large social transfers, is now nearly caught by Spain during the decade.

2.4   Econometric Studies of Unemployment

Does social protection cause unemployment? For some people, the empirical evidence is clear. According to Krugman:

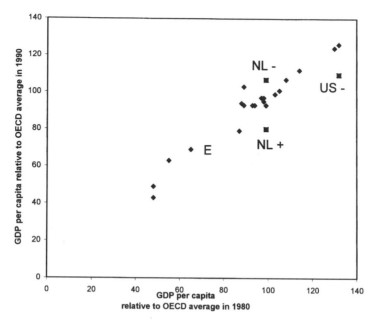

Figure 2.6
GDP per head in 1990 compared with 1980: Predicted in 1990 for United
States and Netherlands. Source: see figure 2.5 and text.

Cross-country regressions, like those of Layard, Nickell and Jackman
(1991), do find that measures of the level of benefits have strong positive effects on long-term averages of national unemployment rates.
(1994, p. 59)

The results of Layard, Nickell, and Jackman (1991) are based
on a statistical regression equation seeking to explain the
average unemployment rate from 1983–1988 in twenty
OECD countries in terms of labor market institutions such as
the benefit variables, spending on active labor market policies,
and wage bargaining institutions. (A more recent study combining the data for 1983–88 with those for 1989–94 has been

carried out by Nickell (1997).) Their work represented a major step forward in that it based the statistical analysis on an explicit theoretical model of the macro labor market. It was not just a case of rounding up the usual suspects and putting them into a regression equation.

The Layard, Nickell, and Jackman study is also distinguished by its treatment of the benefit variables. The problem of the measurement of the size of the welfare state has been extensively discussed in the literature on "welfare effort," where writers on social policy have sought to relate this variable to the success of different countries in reducing poverty or income inequality (for example, Mitchell 1991). However, statistics like those shown in figure 2.1 can be quite misleading. The level of spending relative to GDP does not necessarily provide an indication of the level of benefit per recipient, as is demonstrated in the following decomposition:

spending/GDP = (average benefit/average wage)

$$\times (\text{average wage/GDP per worker})$$

$$\times (\text{recipients/workers}). \qquad (2.3)$$

The first term is usually referred to as the *replacement rate*, the second is the *wage share*, and the third is the *dependency ratio*. So that a spending ratio of 15 percent of GDP may correspond to a replacement rate of 75 percent with a wage share of 60 percent and a dependency ratio of 1/3, or to a replacement rate of 30 percent with a wage share of 75 percent and a dependency ratio of 2/3. Put another way, countries may differ in the extent of needs: one may have a high spending ratio on account of a large dependent population, not on account of a generous social security program. Spending in another country may be low because it is successful in managing its macroeconomy rather than because it attaches low priority to social welfare. This is relevant if it is the generosity of benefit levels which is believed to have an adverse impact on economic behavior, since a high level of welfare state spending does not necessarily imply a high level of generosity.[9]

The distinction between benefit generosity and aggregate spending is important when considering the historical record. In the United Kingdom, aggregate spending, as shown in figure 2.2, has not fallen dramatically, but the generosity of benefits has been reduced in a way not paralleled in other European countries. Two indicators particularly relevant to the fields discussed in this book are the level of the basic state pension and the replacement rate offered by unemployment insurance and assistance. The basic state pension is received almost universally by those over the minimum pension age and is paid at broadly a uniform cash rate. In the past this rate rose more or less in line with incomes elsewhere in the economy, but since the early 1980s it has been indexed only to retail prices, implying that it has fallen as a percentage of average incomes: between 1979 and 1990 it fell from 42 percent of average equivalent income (i.e., income adjusted for differing household composition by an equivalence scale) to around 33 percent. If the policy is continued, it will fall to less than a quarter in 2010. As far as the unemployed are concerned, the replacement rate in the United Kingdom, already low by the standards of Belgium, Germany, and the Netherlands, was significantly reduced between 1981 and 1991, as benefits have been cut back and coverage reduced.

The equation of Layard, Nickell, and Jackman (1991) explaining cross-country variation in unemployment contains measures of both replacement rates and of benefit duration (which affects the recipient rate). They find statistically significant coefficients for both variables, a finding which has been widely cited (for example, in the review for the OECD by

Elmeskov (1993) of the causes of high and persistent unemployment). According to the estimated coefficients, a rise in the replacement ratio of 10 percentage points is associated with a rise in the average (over time) unemployment rate of 1.7 percentage points. An increase in the maximum duration of unemployment benefit of one year is associated with an increase in the unemployment rate of 0.9 percentage points. These are large effects: they mean that Germany, with long benefit duration and a replacement rate of 63 percent, would be predicted to have, on average, an unemployment rate more than 5 percentage points higher than the United States. At the same time, we should bear in mind the confidence intervals surrounding these estimates: the 95 percent confidence interval for the effect of duration is from 0.3 percentage points to 1.5 percentage points.

Attention has been concentrated above on the effects on unemployment, whereas we may be more concerned about the effect on employment, the difference being nonparticipation in the labor force. Nickell (1997) found in his cross-section study that benefits had little impact on employment/population ratios: "[W]hile high benefits lead to high unemployment, they also lead to high participation because they make participation in the labor market more attractive" (p. 67). This will be a theme that recurs in the theoretical chapters.

2.5   Assessing the Findings about Unemployment

The findings of Layard, Nickell, and Jackman differed from those of earlier studies that had identified no relation between benefits and aggregate unemployment. These earlier studies included that by the OECD Employment Outlook in 1991, which related unemployment in 1987 (as a percentage of the population of working age) to the average replacement rate for three different family situations. They concluded that "there is no correlation between this general replacement rate indicator and the overall unemployment rate" (p. 204–208). In the subsequent Jobs Study, the OECD set out three reasons why its earlier findings may have been misleading (1994a, p. 177). There are in fact several reasons for being cautious about drawing firm conclusions:

• causality may be difficult or impossible to establish,

• a more subtle analysis of the timepath of responses may be necessary,

• it may be difficult to isolate from aggregate data the influence of specific benefit programs.

The problem of determining causality has already been considered in relation to growth performance, and applies equally here. It may be that there is a relation between benefit generosity and unemployment, but that this is obscured by both variables being related, in opposite ways, to a third variable. The OECD (1994a) refers to the example that Southern European countries with high levels of agricultural employment, self-employment, and concealed employment may have also high reported unemployment, but the same factors have retarded the development of benefit programs. On the other hand, there may be reverse causation with either sign: countries with low unemployment can "afford" more generous unemployment benefit programs, or countries prone to unemployment "need" more extensive programs (we would not be surprised to find more malaria hospitals in tropical countries).

In seeking to relate country differences in unemployment to differences in benefit variables, we have been implicitly assuming a contemporaneous relationship between social transfers and unemployment, but it may be a dynamic one in the sense that behavior adjusts only with a lag. Lindbeck (1995a, 1995b) has argued that individual responses are influenced by social norms that adapt over time. Initially the welfare state did not affect labor market behavior, but over time people became more willing to live off unemployment benefits and the negative impact began to be important. In order to test this hypothesis, evidence is required about the formation of social norms and their impact on labor market behavior.[10]

In aggregate terms, we need to allow for lagged effects (see, for example, OECD 1994a), but the specification is a matter where we need to exercise considerable care. As emphasized by Layard, Nickell, and Jackman (1991), the welfare state may affect the speed of response to exogenous shocks. Unemployment may have risen initially for reasons unconnected with the welfare state, and these shocks may have affected all countries in much the same way, but, according to this argument, those countries with smaller welfare states responded more quickly. The econometric estimates of Layard, Nickell, and Jackman based on both cross-country and time-series variation bear this out to the extent that the degree of persistence of unemployment depends significantly and positively on the benefit duration variable (but not on the replacement rate). Adjustment is faster in countries where benefits are paid for shorter periods. The dynamic specification of employment models is an aspect that needs to be carefully treated, as in the growth rate studies; indeed, the two may be related in that employment may be adjusting to a moving target (see Karanassou and Snower 1998).

The third reason for caution is that it may be difficult to isolate from aggregate data the specific influence of benefit programs. For instance, let us take the duration of unemployment benefit, to which Layard, Nickell, and Jackman attach great importance: "The unconditional payment of benefits for an indefinite period is clearly a major cause of high European unemployment" (1991, p. 62). Their cross-country data for unemployment in 1983–8 and unemployment benefit duration (in 1985) are plotted in figure 2.7. This immediately brings out several aspects. The first is the concentration of durations on four years. In fact they treat cases with an indefinite period as four years, so that what we have in effect is a distinction between those with time-limited and those with indefinite benefits. It is more a 0/1 difference. Then there is the curious position of the Scandinavian countries, marked by squares rather than diamonds. Curious in that we would expect them to be among the generous, whereas they are shown as having short benefit durations. In fact this seems to be a misreading. According to a comparative study organized by the Dutch Government, "In Sweden it is possible to renew the benefit period by claiming a 'job-offer' before the initial period expires.... This can be repeated over and over again" (Ministry of Social Affairs and Employment 1995, p. 44). The OECD Jobs Study similarly states, "In Denmark, Norway and Sweden, the guarantee for the long-term unemployed of a place on an active labour market programme, which lasts just long enough to generate a new period of benefit entitlement, has made it possible to receive insurance benefits almost indefinitely: Sweden becomes a country with high rather than low benefit entitlements when this is taken into account" (1994, p. 176). If we were to shift Scandinavia to the indefinite category, we would get a rather different picture. Most of Europe would be on the right, with only Italy, Portugal, and Switzerland on the left. There are really two spikes, and there is evidently a lot of variation at both spikes.

Clearly the statistical analysis needs to be more sophisticated than simply eyeing a graph, but equally I believe that one has to ask what lies behind econometric results. How far

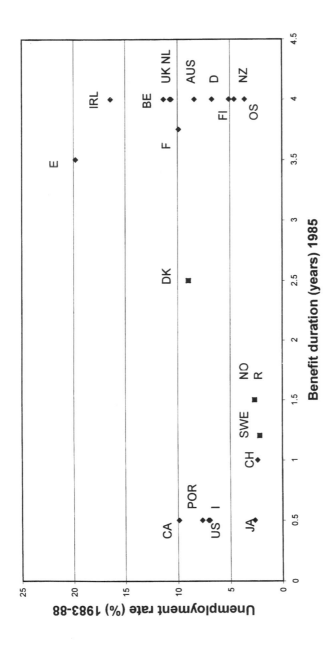

Figure 2.7
Unemployment rates and benefit duration. Source: Layard, Nickell, and Jackman 1991, p. 51.

are we identifying the contribution of the particular policy variable? Can we separate out the impact of benefit duration? It is important to see benefit provisions as forming part of a whole, an idea encapsulated in the title of an article by Freeman called "The Large Welfare State as a System" (1995). Drawing on the NBER-SNS study of Sweden (Freeman, Swedenborg, and Topel 1997), Freeman concludes that it is "a highly inter-related welfare state and economy in which many parts fit together ... in ways that maintained high employment and wage compression, that offset work disincentives from welfare benefits and high taxes" (1995, p. 18).

Among the other parts of the story are "off-budget activities" (Saunders 1986), such as the regulation of the private sector or minimum wage legislation. Recently attention has turned to mandating the employer provision of benefits, shifting the burden from the state budget to firm payrolls. This has evident attractions for policymakers: "In an era of tight fiscal budget constraints, mandating employer provision of workplace benefits to employees is an attractive means for a government to finance its policy agenda" (Gruber 1994a, p. 622). The economic consequences of such benefits cannot, however, be ignored simply because they have been shifted to employers. They may also have fiscal implications. Not only may they reduce taxable profits, but also they may be accompanied by fiscal concessions. It is of course open to question how far such mandating of benefits is a binding constraint (on employer-related health insurance in the United States, see Gruber 1994b).

The interrelations of the system are one reason I am not convinced that one can learn a lot from simply cross-country evidence. Countries differ in a variety of ways, and one cannot easily pull out one variable as responsible for the observed differences in performance.

2.6   Conclusion

Aggregate cross-country evidence, interesting though it may be, cannot on its own provide a reliable guide to the likely consequences of rolling back the welfare state. Fifteen years ago Maddison stated:

It is difficult to reach strong conclusions on the influence of the welfare state on economic development because the evidence does not warrant them. Strong judgements on the question are influenced mainly by ideological positions, or predictions about what might happen in the future. (1984, p. 83)

Since then, we have seen some of the future, but the position is not a great deal clearer. There are still grounds for agnosticism. Sandmo, for example, after a review of the aggregate empirical evidence about a possible trade-off between growth and social security, concluded that "the adoption of the Nordic model of social security does not have catastrophic consequences for economic growth, nor is it a guarantee of economic success" (1995, p. 4). He goes on to say that

theoretical hypotheses and data analysis at this level do not reveal the more basic structural features of the economy. To understand the connections that there *may* be, we need first of all to look into the theoretical underpinnings of the tradeoff hypothesis, and secondly to consider whether there may be some arguments that point in the opposite direction. (1995, p. 4)

I read this passage after embarking on this study, but it provides a clear statement of what I am seeking to do in the remainder of these lectures.

Appendix:
Studies of Growth Rate and Social Transfers

Study	Landau 1985	Korpi 1985	Weede 1986	McCallum and Blais 1987	Castles and Dowrick 1990
Dependent variable	Real per capita GDP Pooled time series/cross-section	Real per capita GDP Mixed time series/cross-section	Real GDP and real per capita GDP Pooled time series/cross-section	Real GDP Pooled time series/cross-section	Real per capita GDP Pooled time series/cross-section
Period	Annual growth rates 1952–1976	Period 1950–73 and sub-periods 1950–59, 60–66, 67–73, 73–79	Period 1960–82 and sub-periods 1960–68, 68–73, 73–79, 79–82	Sub-periods 1960–67, 67–73, 73–79, 79–83	Sub-periods 1960–68, 69–73, 74–79, 80–85
Countries	16 OECD (inc. Japan)	17 OECD (exc. Japan)	19 OECD (inc. Japan)	17 OECD inc. Japan	18 OECD or 17 exc. Japan
Model and variables	Model (2.2), with human capital (education), GDP (catchup), terms of trade (openness), country intercepts	Total effect, but controls for % labor force in agriculture or GDP per capita (catchup)	Total effect, but controls for % agricultural employment, age of democracy	Model (2.2) but exc. investment, with log GDP per capita (catchup), modernization, growth of govt exp/GDP, subperiod dummies	Model (2.2), with log GDP per capita (catchup), sclerosis, sub-period dummies

	General government transfers (OECD national accounts)/GDP (different deflators)	ILO social security expenditure/GDP	OECD social security transfers/GDP (from Historical Statistics)	OECD social security transfers/GDP (from Historical Statistics) adjusted for % aged 65+	OECD social expenditure less health and education, extended 1982–85 using OECD national accounts
Definition of transfer variable*					
Coefficient on WS (standard error)	0.012 IV, HS corrected (0.037)	1950–73: 0.193 (0.050) 1973–79: 0.182 (0.064) Similar with catchup variable	−0.21 (n/a) or −0.19 (n/a) exc. Japan and Switzerland	0.12 for 1960–79 (0.03) $0.31\,WS - 0.0092\,WS^2$ (0.09) (0.0031) for 1960–83	Controlling for emp and inv 5.24 or 7.45 (3.54) (3.53) Not controlling exc. Japan 1960–68 −1.01 or 1.93 (3.74) (3.45)
Effect of 5 percentage point reduction in WS	Not significant at 5% level	0.9 percentage point reduction in annual growth rate	1 percentage point increase in annual growth rate	0.5 percentage point reduction in annual growth rate (1960–79 estimate) zero at WS = 16.8% with 1960–83 estimates	Controlled estimates: 0.3–0.4 percentage point reduction in annual growth rate of total factor productivity

Appendix (continued)

Study	Weede 1991	Sala-i-Martin 1992	Nordström (1992)	Hansson and Henrekson 1994	Persson and Tabellini 1994
Dependent variable	Real GDP, per capita GDP, and per person employed Pooled time series/cross-section	Real per capita GDP Cross-section	Real GDP Cross-section	Real private output in 14 industry/service sectors Cross-country/cross-industry	Real per capita GDP Cross-section
Period	Sub-periods 1960–68, 68–73, 73–79, 79–85	1970–85	1977–89	1970–87	1960–85
Countries	19 OECD inc. Japan	74 countries world wide	14 OECD inc. Japan or 13 exc. Japan	14 OECD inc. Japan	13 OECD inc. Japan
Model and variables	Total effect and productivity per person employed, with agricultural employment, age of democracy	Model (2.2), but exc. employment, with log GDP per capita (catchup)	Total effect	Model (2.2), with catchup variable	Total effect, with GDP per capita (catchup variable), % attending primary school

	OECD social security transfers/GDP (from His-torical Statistics)	Public transfers	Other current transfers in OECD National Accounts	OECD social security transfers/GDP² (from Historical Statistics)	OECD social expenditure series/GDP (pensions + unemployment comp. + other social exp)
Definition of transfer variable*					
Coefficient on WS (standard error)	Productivity results: −0.11 (n/a) or −0.084 (n/a) exc. Japan	0.111 (0.054)	−0.120 (0.034) Table 1, col 2 (and similar results for other specifications) −0.119 (0.039) exc. Japan Table 2, col 2	−0.063 (0.036) Table 4, eqn (xi) for WS average 1965–82 or −0.050 (0.035) eqn (xii) for WS average 1970–87	−6.723 (5.396) Table 8, eqn (iii)
Effect of 5 percentage point reduction in WS	0.5 percentage point increase in annual growth rate of productivity	0.6 percentage point reduction in annual growth rate	0.6 percentage point increase in annual growth rate	Not significant at 5% level (but significant negative coefficient for total transfers)	0.3 percentage point increase in annual growth rate

Note: *measured in percentage points apart from Castles and Dowrick 1990 and Persson and Tabellini 1994, which are measured as fractions of GDP.

3　　　　　　　Equilibrium Models of
　　　　　　　　the Labor Market

I now begin to consider the theoretical basis for propositions that may link the scale of welfare state spending to economic performance. What are the theoretical reasons why we may expect rolling back social transfers to improve the operation of the economy? Or the reverse? In the previous chapter, I distinguished between a relationship linking the scale of spending to the level of performance indicators and a relationship linking the scale of spending to their rate of growth. Rolling back the welfare state would, on the first basis, produce a once-for-all change in performance indicators; on the second basis, it would lead to a change that becomes magnified over time. In this and the next chapter I am concerned with the *levels relationship*; in chapters 6 and 7 I consider the growth of the economy.

3.1　A Simple Competitive Equilibrium Model

In chapter 1, I suggested that the theoretical framework adopted in much analysis of the welfare state remains rooted in a model of perfectly competitive and perfectly clearing markets. The following section describes an elementary competitive equilibrium model applied to the analysis of the impact of a social transfer program and the implications of scaling back expenditure.

In this simple model, transfer payments are made to a recipient group, fixed in size as a fraction of the total population, who are not in the labor force and are referred to as "pensioners." The remainder of the population, of working age, either work in the market or in home production. The proportion of working age is denoted by n. There are therefore three groups: pensioners (proportion $(1 - n)$), those in market work, and those producing home output. A social security tax at rate t is levied on the earnings of those in market work in order to finance the transfer to the pensioners (it would make no difference in this model if the tax were levied on the employer). Firms produce a single output, and the demand for labor by competitive firms is determined by equating the value marginal product of labor with the total wage cost per worker. There is no uncertainty, and firms are correctly confident about their plans. The competitive labor supply by workers depends on their alternative opportunity of home production. As the wage rises, a larger fraction of individuals prefer market work. I shall talk in terms of "individuals," since their household circumstances play no role in the analysis, although in reality this is important. According to Gregg and Wadsworth (1996), variation across countries in worklessness among households is only weakly correlated with the rates of unemployment for individuals.

We have therefore a simple supply and demand model of the labor market. Competition ensures that people are efficiently allocated between home production and market production. To make this more concrete, let us suppose that the value of output produced using L workers is denoted by the price times the output $Y(L)$. (The production function is assumed to be strictly increasing, and strictly concave, in L.)

Profit-maximizing competitive firms behave such that

$$Y'(L) = w, \qquad (3.1)$$

where w denotes the real wage cost. Inverting this relationship gives the labor demand as a function of the real wage. For illustration, we may take the example of the Cobb-Douglas production function already introduced in chapter 2:

$$Y = AK^\beta L^{1-\beta}, \qquad (3.2)$$

where K denotes capital and A the level of labor productivity (both assumed constant until chapter 6). This generates a labor demand function:

$$L^D = Cw^{-1/\beta}, \qquad (3.3)$$

where C is a constant.

Individual workers are assumed to be equally productive in market work but to differ in their productivity in home employment (home output is valued at the same price as market output). There is a maximum total labor force, n (if we normalize the total population at 1), but a fraction of potential workers prefer home employment. This latter decision is assumed to be based on whether the value of home output, x, is greater or less than the real net of tax wage rate, $w(1-t)$; that is,

$$x > \text{ or } < w(1-t). \qquad (3.4)$$

If the distribution function of home output (i.e., the proportion who produce x or less) is $F(x)$, then the labor supply is

$$L^S = F[w(1-t)]n; \qquad (3.5)$$

that is, those who produce home output less than $w(1-t)$ and therefore choose to work in the market.

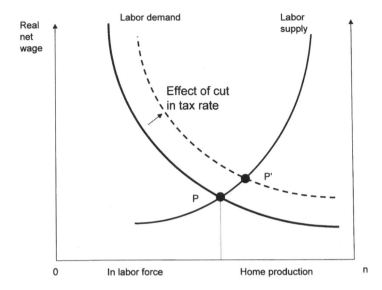

Figure 3.1
Competitive model of labor market

This model of the aggregate labor market is depicted in figure 3.1. The real net wage, which determines the supply, is
measured on the vertical axis. In the demand relation, the cost
to the employer is the net wage divided by $(1 - t)$, so the
demand curve is determined by equating $(1 - t)Y'(L)$ to the
net wage. There is a competitive equilibrium at the point P
where the wage w is such that supply and demand are equated.

Suppose now that we examine the effect of reducing the
average transfer payment to the pensioner population, denoted
by T per head. It is assumed that the government budget has
to balance so that the value of payments equals the social
security tax paid; that is,

$$(1 - n)T = ntwF[w(1 - t)]. \tag{3.6}$$

The relationship between T and t may be nonmonotonic: where the revenue from the payroll tax begins to fall beyond a certain point as the fall in F more than offsets the rise in t on the right-hand side of equation (3.6). In such a case—the celebrated Laffer curve—cutting the tax rate may have both efficiency and equity advantages. Here I assume that we are not in this region and that reductions in the tax rate lead to reductions in the transfer.

The effect of reducing the social security payroll tax is to reduce the cost to the employer at any given net wage, so the demand curve shifts to the right. There is no other change. From figure 3.1 it may be seen that the equilibrium moves from P to P'. In part, there is a rise in the net wage rate; in part, there is a rise in the equilibrium level of market employment, and hence market output. A reduction in the rate of transfer to the dependant population (which could take the form either of reducing the transfer per head or of reducing the size of the population considered eligible) which lowers the necessary tax rate leads to a rise in measured output. In this case we have a negative levels relationship between the scale of the welfare state and GDP.

3.2   Issues Raised

The model just described is extremely simplified, but it serves to identify a number of issues.

GDP versus Welfare

First, it is open to question whether GDP is really the appropriate performance indicator in this context. Along with the reduced labor supply comes increased home production. The professors who paint their own houses rather than write books are still contributing to output. This is not just an accounting point. Much of public debate confuses the potential damage that taxes may do by (1) distorting the working of the market and (2) reducing output (or employment, or investment, or some other target economic variable). The distortion in the simple model set out above arises from the "wedge" between the cost of labor to the employer (w) and the opportunity cost to the employee (x). The distortion would be eliminated if t were zero. On the other hand, this would not maximize market output.

It may be convenient to use observed GDP as an aggregate indicator of well-being, ignoring nonpaid labor, but the distinction is important. If it is being argued that the welfare state is driving people out of the market economy, then we should be told whether this is undesirable because it leads to an inefficient allocation of resources or because it reduces GDP. The numerical measure of the cost may be very different. The distortionary loss from a small tax, for example, is only second-order, whereas the output effect is first-order. This distinction has been drawn clearly by Lindbeck, who argues that we should focus not on "the 'positive economics issue' of whether work effort falls or rises in response to some government action, but rather ... on the 'welfare economics issue' of whether deviations are created, or raised, between the social and private return on (marginal) work effort" (1981, p. 31).

As he recognizes, however, social judgments may not be based on purely welfarist concerns. The considerations that enter social decision criteria may not be confined to individual welfare levels. Governments may legitimately be interested, for instance, in the level of economic development that a country has attained. For this purpose, GDP may be a reasonable, if crude, first approximation. In these lectures I pay most attention to output, or employment, or, in a dynamic formulation, the rate of growth of GDP, in view of their political salience.

Tax Cost versus Specific Impact

The cost in lost output, or reduced welfare, arises on account of the existence of taxation: it is a tax cost argument. The fact that the reason for the tax is financing transfers is not as such material. The welfare state may represent a particularly large item in the budget, but the tax cost is the same euro for euro as if the spending were on overseas aid or military defence. By the same token, tax expenditures have an identical impact to that of direct spending. (A number of empirical studies have added tax expenditures to direct social security payments when calculating welfare effort: for example, Gilbert and Moon 1988.) Allowances against income taxation may play the same role as cash transfers in that both increase the necessary tax rate. A higher tax exemption for the elderly reduces the overall tax receipts, as do child tax allowances. Replacing child income tax allowances by a cash child benefit may appear to increase the size of the welfare state, but does not necessarily affect the tax rate that has to be levied on income.

It is important to distinguish this general tax cost argument from arguments that are specific to the particular form of spending. Going back to the quotation from Drèze and Malinvaud at the start of this book, we can see that their second criticism of welfare state programs is that they "increase the size of government at a risk of inefficiency; their funding enhances the amount of revenue to be raised" (1994, p. 95). (The third is that they increase public deficits). Cuts in the transfer would allow the tax rate to be reduced, but the same may be true if other forms of government expenditure or tax expenditures were contracted. Rolling back the defence budget would also reduce the taxes that have to be levied.

More interesting in the present context are arguments pointing to specific features of welfare state spending that have an impact on economic performance, as illustrated by Drèze and Malinvaud's first criticism of the welfare state that "measures of income protection or social insurance introduce undesired rigidities in the functioning of labour markets" (1994, p. 95). We are now concerned with the relative desirability of different types of government spending. The question is one of *differential expenditure* analysis, to use Musgrave's terminology (Musgrave 1959). The significance of this distinction may be seen if we allow the transfer to affect the working of the labor market other than through simply the tax rate. I have assumed above that the recipient population is fixed in size, but it could be influenced by the payment of the transfer. Suppose now that people of working age can receive the transfer while engaged in home production. (The rules of transfer programs may place obstacles in the way of such behavior, as discussed in the next chapter.) As a result, the supply curve is to the left of that shown in figure 3.1, since those who can receive the transfer now compare the net wage with $(x + T)$. Reducing the transfer now shifts the supply curve to the right, in addition to the effect of the tax cut. The level of market output rises further than if there were simply the tax cost. The wedge between the value of market output and the net benefit to the worker narrows for those able to claim while working at home, and there is a further gain in welfare. (It may be noted in passing that a basic income payable to all, whether working or not, and whether in paid or home production, would be neutral with respect to the labor supply decision.)

Put differently, social transfers have been criticized in two ways. The first is that they add to the financing problems of the government; the second is that, even if free, they adversely affect the working of the labor or other markets. The first of these criticisms can be countered by proposing alternative expenditure cuts, but the second requires us to focus on the impact of the transfers. In what follows, I give most attention to this second aspect: the specific impact of social transfers. Compared with the extensive literature on the possible disincentive effects of taxation, the impact of cash transfers has been relatively less researched, and it is useful in analytical terms to keep the effects separate. Changes in transfers are of themselves of considerable policy interest. If the second line of criticism of the welfare state is valid, then a reduction in benefit levels or coverage will have positive effects, even without reference to any reductions in tax or social security contribution rates. This is the policy experiment I commonly consider in the analysis that follows.

Contributions and Benefits

The social transfer program considered so far is purely redistributive between people: the taxpayer and the beneficiaries are distinct people. To the extent that the taxpayer perceives a link between the taxes paid and future benefits, the economic effect is moderated. This can be the case with a contributory social insurance scheme, where benefits are linked at an individual level to contributions made (for example, where they are proportional). In that situation, those in paid employment base the labor supply decision on comparing the value of home output, x, with the wage rate, net of tax *and* expected benefit from future receipt of the transfer:

$$x > \text{ or } < w(1 - t) + \psi T, \tag{3.7}$$

where ψ is the present value placed on the transfer, T. To the extent that ψ is positive, the scaling down of social insurance has a less marked impact on the level of output. The supply curve now shifts to the left since people reckon that they are losing future benefits, so that market work is less attractive at any given net wage. If $tw = \psi T$, then the gross wage can remain unchanged. The working of the economy is not in this case affected by the existence of actuarily fair transfers.

This can be oversold. When Lloyd George introduced National Insurance in the United Kingdom in 1911, he used the phrase "ninepence for fourpence" to persuade people of the merits of the scheme, the grounds being that the employee contributed fourpence but the employer threepence and the state twopence (Grigg 1978, p. 325). Eliding the fact that these contributions too should enter the equation was clearly not legitimate, however successful it was as political rhetoric. But even counting all contributions social insurance may return the full amount. Put another way, it is open to countries to operate different forms of social insurance where these are actuarily neutral. The existence of social insurance need not affect competitiveness, in that the effect on the equilibrium value of w depends only on the net value. If tw equals ψT, then the scale of the scheme does not matter. In an aggregate study the size of the welfare state would be irrelevant.

When considering the value placed on future receipt of social transfers, an important element is the political risk associated with the continuance of the scheme (see, for example, Diamond 1993 and Lindbeck 1995a). There is here an obvious circle. Expectations of benefit cuts cause people to discount future entitlements and treat social security contributions as a pure tax. This leads to adverse economic impacts, which validate the doubts about the financial security of the scheme and strengthen calls for its scaling back. As long as confidence is retained the social security scheme may be quite viable, but once doubts have come to be held we may have embarked on a trajectory that leads to inevitable rolling back of the welfare state. The potential responsibility of economists for such a development is evident. If economists claim that the current welfare state is unsustainable, thus causing a fall in public confidence, then the prediction becomes self-fulfilling. I return in chapter 5 to the role of the economist as actor rather than observer.

What Is the Alternative?

Reference to the benefit side of transfer programs raises the issue of the alternative to the welfare state. Those advocating the rolling back of the welfare state normally assume that other provisions would take its place, either as part of accompanying government reforms or spontaneously. Critics of the public pay-as-you-go pension, for example, typically wish to see a better targeting of state spending, with the public pension being subject to a test of means. This means that we are being asked to compare two different benefit structures: for example, a uniform payment with one that is reduced where there is other income. The budget constraint for the individual household is changed. This is the alternative considered below in chapter 6.

A second alternative is private provision. In the case of retirement pensions, state provision would be replaced by mandatory contributions to private pensions. These are often treated as being equivalent, apart from their mandatory nature, to private savings. There may, however, be important differences for the capital market, notably those that arise from savings being channeled through financial institutions such as pension funds rather than individual shareholdings, as discussed in chapter 7. Private, or trade union, provision can also arise in the case of unemployment insurance, and this is addressed in chapter 4. In each case we have to ask how the alternative would affect economic performance.

Stock Taking

The competitive equilibrium model provides a simple framework within which we can see how scaling down social transfers may increase GDP. It brings out the need to distinguish between output and welfare, to keep separate the charge that high taxes reduce output from the charge that the adverse effect arises from specific features of the social transfer system, to recognize the possible connection between taxes and benefits under a social insurance program, and to consider the alternative that would replace state provision. The reader should note that in the rest of the book I shall be giving particular weight to output and its growth, and to the specific features of social transfers rather than the tax financing costs.

The competitive model is highly stylized, but that in itself is not an objection. What *is* seriously worrying is that the theoretical model incorporates none of the imperfections that characterize actual economies. We need to move beyond this miniature Arrow-Debreu general equilibrium system. In particular, we need to allow for unemployment, which is one of the main contingencies for which the welfare state has sought to provide.

3.3 Models of Unemployment

The fact of large-scale unemployment in Europe means that it is self-evident that we need to consider a model of the economy that allows for its existence, but it is also apparent from the literature on European unemployment that there is little agreement about its causes. Lindbeck (1993), for example, lists the following possible microeconomic explanations: government controls (minimum wage legislation), social norms against underbidding of wages, trade unions, efficiency wages, and insider/outsider theories. As he notes, these theories may be complementary rather than competing. Layard, Nickell, and Jackman (1991) in their multicountry study of unemployment include, in addition to the benefit variables described in chapter 2, the proportion of employees with less than two years tenure (taken as a measure of employment adjustment costs), a measure of the degree of corporatism (or a measure of employer/union power), and wage inertia (measured by contract length, degree of indexation, and degree of synchronization of contracts). Bean in his survey of European unemployment concludes that "there does not seem to be any single cause of the rise in European unemployment" (1994, p. 615).

As a result, we cannot simply take off the shelf an agreed model within which to examine the role of unemployment insurance. This in itself may lead to different conclusions—a warning the reader should bear in mind when considering the models presented in this book. In the rest of this chapter I look at a model of permanent job terminations, imperfect matching of vacancies and jobseekers, and trade union bargaining over wages.

The model is influenced both by the current macroeconomic literature and by the historical emergence of unemployment as part of the transition to a modern, industrialized economy. Unemployment is a relatively recent concept. According to Garraty (1978, p. 4), the word did not come into general use in English until the mid-1890s and its first appearance in the U.S. Department of Labor Bulletin was in 1913 (Garraty 1978, p. 122). Its recent origins are well captured in the title of the book by Salais, Baverez, and Reynaud: L'invention du chômage. As it is described by Piore in a review of the book:

The modern concept of unemployment derives from one particular employment relationship, that of the large, permanent manufacturing establishment. Employment in such institutions involves a radical separation in time and space from family and leisure time activity.... When employment ties of this kind are severed, there is an empty space in the worker's life. (1987, p. 1836)

Unemployment is associated with a labor market situation where employment is a $0/1$ phenomenon. The move from the traditional agricultural sector to modern industry may be characterized—in an oversimplified way—as moving from a lower-level income, with underemployment, to one where the wage was higher but subject to the "catastrophic" hazard of total unemployment. A depression left industrial workers totally without resources; they could not fall back on home production or on the mixture of part-time employment and self-employment that was found in rural society. Unemployment was seen as an inevitable part of modern industrial economies. As Engels wrote in his *Condition of the Working Class in England*: "Industry must always have a reserve of unemployed workers" (quoted in Garraty 1978, p. 105). In our model we have therefore three states (the pensioner population is not taken into account here, so $n = 1$): An employee in the modern sector is either engaged at wage w, unemployed with no wage, or self-employed in the traditional sector. Self-employment corresponds to the sector treated as home production in section 3.1, and the distribution function is assumed to be such that a proportion $F(x)$ of the population produce x or less if self-employed. This may involve periods of underemployment, which are allowed for in the calculation of x but are not covered by any benefits.

In this model, unemployment insurance may be functional in the development of the modern sector of the economy. People have to be induced to enter the employment relationship, with the attendant risk of total loss of income. This risk is represented formally by supposing that any worker faces at all times a probability, δ, that his or her job will be involuntarily terminated. An increase in job insecurity, as has been perceived in many OECD countries in recent years, is captured by an increase in δ. On becoming redundant a person may seek another vacancy, and, even though these exist, this process may take some time. In order to simplify the analysis, strong (and not necessarily realistic) assumptions are made about the possible labor market transitions. It is assumed that recruitment by firms takes place only from the stock of unemployed; there is no recruitment of those engaged in self-employment or those already in employment. (For a critique of this assumption, see Lindbeck and Snower 1990). The self-employed, for example, cannot compete for modern sector jobs because of the geographical separation or because they have to be available for work.

The probability of moving from unemployment to paid work is assumed equal for all unemployed. It depends on the number of vacancies and on the matching of the unemployed to vacant jobs, which is assumed to be imperfect so that not all jobs are filled instantaneously. I assume that the matching function, with U unemployed and V vacancies, takes the special form such that the number of matches is (see for example Blanchard and Diamond 1990):

$$M = m\sqrt{(UV)}, \tag{3.8}$$

so that the rate of outward flow from unemployment is

$$M/U = m\sqrt{(V/U)} \equiv \mu. \tag{3.9}$$

This is the instantaneous probability for an unemployed person of finding a job.

At any time, the average number of job terminations is δL, where L is the total employment in the modern sector. In equilibrium this is equal to the number of matches

$$\delta L = M = m\sqrt{(UV)}, \tag{3.10}$$

so that we can express U relative to L:

$$U = (\delta L/m)\sqrt{(U/V)} = \delta L/\mu. \tag{3.11}$$

Total frictional unemployment is proportional to L, the size of the modern sector, where the factor of proportionality depends on U/V, which is an index of pressure in the labor market.

Why should workers be willing to wait for modern sector jobs in the circumstances envisaged above? After all, in the absence of unemployment benefit, they have no income while unemployed, and they could be self-employed with a positive income. In order to answer this, we need to calculate the valuation of the state of being unemployed. In making this calculation, we assume that workers are risk neutral. This assumption, maintained throughout the lectures, means that the model is not an appropriate vehicle to discuss the role of actuarial private insurance. (On this important dimension of the welfare state, see, for example, Sinn 1981, 1995, and 1996, Sandmo 1991, Barr 1992, Atkinson 1991, and Bird 1998.) It is also assumed that workers have an infinite horizon (again, not a particularly realistic assumption, but one that is commonly made) and discount future income at an exogenously fixed interest rate, r. I examine the situation in which we are in a stationary equilibrium, with wages, the interest rate, the job termination rate, and the outflow rate from unemployed all expected to remain unchanged over time. (Alternatively, we could assume myopic expectations.) Under these assumptions, the valuation, Ω_i, placed on a particular state i of unemployment or employment is of the form:

$$r\Omega_i = \text{flow benefits} + \text{expected capital gain.} \tag{3.12}$$

This valuation formula parallels that for stock market values used in chapter 7; its application to labor markets is explained by, among others, Shapiro and Stiglitz (1984, p. 436), who sketch a formal derivation. In the case of the unemployed, in the absence of benefits there is simply the expected capital gain, which is given by

$$r\Omega_U = [\Omega_J - \Omega_U]\mu, \tag{3.13}$$

where Ω_J denotes the value of holding a modern sector job, and the probability is derived from (3.9).

People are assumed to be able to move freely out of unemployment into self-employment. The present value of output in self-employment is x/r, so that there is a critical value

$$x^* = r\Omega_U \tag{3.14}$$

such that a proportion $F(x^*)$ of the population choose to participate in the modern sector.

What is the value of a modern sector job? Under the same assumptions about workers' horizons, etc., the expected present value of a job paying wage w is such that

$$r\Omega_J = w - \delta(\Omega_J - \Omega_U). \tag{3.15}$$

Equation (3.15) shows that the flow benefits of the job are attenuated by the risk of job termination (a job forever would be worth w/r). Using (3.14), we can solve for

$$\Omega_J = [w/r + (x^*/r)\delta/r]/(1 + \delta/r)$$

$$= \Omega_U + (w - x^*)/(r + \delta). \tag{3.16}$$

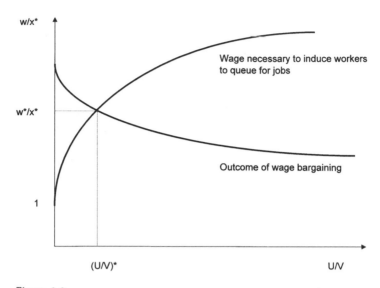

Figure 3.2
Determination of wage in unionized labor market

Substituting from (3.14) and (3.16) into (3.13), we obtain the relation that must hold in equilibrium between the wage rate and the marginal value of self-employment, x^* (eliminating Ω_J and Ω_U and substituting for μ from (3.11)):

$$w = x^*[1 + ((r + \delta)/m)\sqrt{(U/V)}]. \tag{3.17}$$

The necessary wage depends negatively on the effectiveness of matching (m) and positively on the degree of insecurity of employment (δ), but also on the state of the labor market (U/V), as is illustrated by the upward-sloping curve in figure 3.2, which shows the modern sector wage relative to x^* on the vertical axis and U/V on the horizontal axis. We cannot therefore conclude that wages are higher, the more insecure is employment, since (U/V) is endogenous.

Equation (3.17) may in fact be seen as representing the "supply side." The higher U/V, the longer it takes to find a job, and the greater the wage required to induce people to queue. We have now to ask about the demand side; the next section examines the case where there is collective bargaining between employers and trade unions.

3.4 Trade Unions and Unemployment

With the industrialization of Western economies came also the development of trade unions. Like the welfare state, they have not received good press from economists. When unemployment began to rise in Western Europe, it was frequently attributed to the increased union bargaining power following a long postwar period of high employment. This section describes a situation where the presence of trade unions leads to a wedge between the wage in the market economy and the opportunity cost in terms of self-employment.

Trade unions and employers are assumed to bargain over the wage rate, w, in the market economy, in the knowledge that the labor demand function is given by equation (3.3). This is a "right to manage" model where firms determine employment rather than both employment and wages being determined by collective bargaining. The wage is set separately at each individual point in time. Following the standard assumption in the labor economics literature (for example, Booth 1995, p. 125), the outcome is assumed to be the generalized Nash bargaining solution, where employers and unions maximize

$$\Pi^\zeta\{L(\Omega_J - \Omega_U)\}, \tag{3.18}$$

where ζ is a positive parameter measuring the relative bargaining power of the employers, and where the union maxi-

mizes the difference in total expected present value from the
employment of L workers at wage w, compared with their being unemployed. The first-order condition (it may be verified
that the second-order conditions are satisfied) is found by dif-
ferentiating the logarithm of (3.18) with respect to w:

$$(\zeta/\Pi)\partial\Pi/\partial w + (1/L)\partial L/\partial w$$

$$+ (1/[\Omega_J - \Omega_U])\partial[\Omega_J - \Omega_U]/\partial w = 0. \tag{3.19}$$

The derivative of profits with respect to w is equal to $-L$. In
the case of the Cobb-Douglas production function, the elastic-
ity of labor demand is $(1/\beta)$, and the share of profits relative
to wages is $\beta/(1-\beta)$. The third term can be obtained from
the second equation in (3.16). Multiplying by w, the expression (3.19) can therefore be simplified to yield:

$$\zeta(1-\beta)/\beta + 1/\beta - w/(w-x^*) = 0 \quad \text{(see Booth, p. 125).} \tag{3.20}$$

This can be rewritten:

$$w = x^*[1 + (\beta/(1-\beta))/(1+\zeta)], \tag{3.21}$$

so that the negotiated wage is, as we might expect, larger, the
larger is the share of capital (β) and the smaller is the relative
strength of employers (ζ). The differential has a maximum
value of $1/(1-\beta)$ when ζ equals zero, which is the case of the
monopoly union. It is reasonable to suppose that relative bargaining strength varies with the state of the labor market, as
measured by U/V. The more slack the labor market, the less
the bargaining power of the union. This is assumed in figure
3.2, where the downward-sloping curve shows the negotiated
wage as a multiple of x^*.

The equilibrium U/V ratio is that which solves equations
(3.17) and (3.21)—see figure 3.2—and this determines the

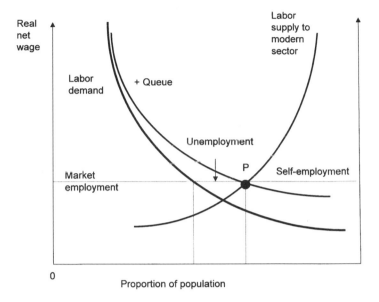

Figure 3.3
Wages and employment in unionized economy

equilibrium ratio of the wage to x^*, denoted by w^*/x^*. Having solved for the ratio, we can now obtain the market-clearing level of x^*. The demand for labour is given by $L^D\{(w^*/x^*).x^*\}$, which is a downward-sloping function of x^*. For the equilibrium value of U/V, the number of unemployed is proportional to L^D (see equation (3.11)). Adding this to labor demand gives the augmented labor demand curve, including the queue unemployment, shown in figure 3.3. The labor market equilibrium condition is

$$[1 + (\delta/m)\sqrt{(U/V)}]L^D\{(w^*/x^*).x^*\} = F[x^*], \qquad (3.22)$$

where the right-hand side is the supply function of labor. Comparing the situation with the frictionless model of section

3.1, for any given wage paid in the market sector, the counterpart self-employment (home) production is lower, on account of the bargained differential, causing the supply of labor to the market to be lower. The wage w is certainly higher, since the demand curve has also shifted outward, on account of the job queue. Employment and output in the market sector are lower than if the labor market cleared without friction and there were no union power.

The model described above serves to illustrate how even a relatively limited modification of the assumptions introduces significant complexity. It is, however, the greater richness of the model that allows us to examine the impact of social transfers in a way that recognizes their distinctive features.

3.5 Unemployment Benefit

Those who attribute unemployment to trade union bargaining power often suggest that it combines with the welfare state to intensify the adverse impact of transfers on the labor market. Moving away from a competitively functioning labor market, introducing union bargaining power may be expected, therefore, to provide an efficiency justification for rolling back social transfers.[11] In contrast to the model of section 3.1, a cut in benefit may reduce unemployment even if there is no change in the payroll tax.

To set this out more formally, we add unemployment benefit to the right-hand side of equation (3.13) for the valuation placed on the state of unemployment:[12]

$$r\Omega_U = [\Omega_J - \Omega_U]\mu + b, \tag{3.13'}$$

where it is assumed that the benefit is financed by a social security tax at rate t on earnings, as earlier. The term w is similarly multiplied by $(1 - t)$ in equation (3.15). It is assumed

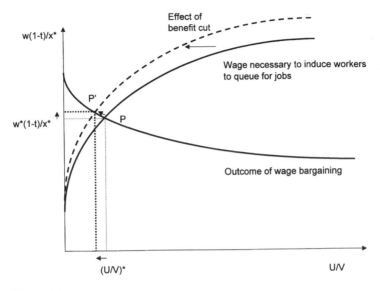

Figure 3.4
Effect on wages and job queue of cut in unemployment benefit

that workers expect benefits and taxes to remain unchanged over time.

We now obtain

$$w(1-t)/x^* = 1 + (1 - b/x^*)(r+\delta)/m)\sqrt{(U/V)}]. \qquad (3.17')$$

If we view figure 3.2 as being drawn with the relative net wage $(w(1-t)/x^*)$ on the vertical axis, then the unemployment benefit causes the upward-sloping curve to rotate clockwise around the point on the vertical axis. Conversely, the reduction of an already existing benefit causes the curve to rotate in the opposite direction (see figure 3.4). Other things equal, queuing for a job becomes less attractive, so that the wage required rises.

The tax on wages affects wage bargaining, since unions are assumed to be concerned with the value of a job net of tax, and the earlier assumptions yield

$$w(1 - t) = x^*[1 + (\beta/(1 - \beta))/(1 + \zeta)]. \tag{3.21'}$$

The wage is bargained in net terms, so that the downward-sloping curve in figure 3.4 is unaffected. With the assumptions made, the level of benefit does not enter directly into the wage bargain, a point to which I later return.

From this analysis, we can see the predicted impact of scaling back unemployment benefit. If the government reduces the level of benefits, this makes waiting for a union job less attractive. In figure 3.4 the upward-sloping curve rotates in a counterclockwise direction, and the equilibrium shifts from P to P'. In order that equilibrium be restored on the supply side, the length of the queue (U/V) has to fall and the ratio $w(1 - t)/x^*$ has to increase. The mix between these two responses depends on the relative slopes. If relative bargaining power remains much the same, then most of the response is via (U/V); if the bargaining power is sensitive to (U/V), then more is reflected in the net wage ratio.

Transposing this to the wage/employment diagram, we can see that if the bargaining power of unions is unaffected by changes in (U/V) (the wage bargaining curve in figure 3.4 is horizontal), as assumed in Atkinson 1995, then the effect of the scaling back of benefits is a shift to the left of the "total" demand curve including those in the job queue. This reduces x^* and hence leads to an increase in market employment; self-employment also increases. This effect is reinforced to the extent that the benefit cut allows a reduction in the social security tax rate, since the labor demand depends on the gross wage. The demand curve shifts to the right with a reduction in

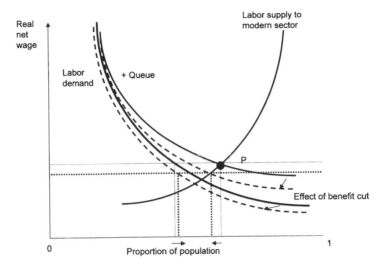

Figure 3.5
Effect on wages and employment of cut in unemployment benefit

the tax rate. But even without changes in the payroll tax, the level of market employment is increased by a cut in benefits.

This picture of falling job queue and rising labor demand in response to a benefit and tax cut has to be modified to the extent that the cut in benefits leads to a rise in the $w(1 - t)/x^*$ ratio, as shown in figure 3.4. Suppose we consider the specific impact of the benefit cut (holding the tax rate constant). As noted earlier, people have to be induced to enter the search for employment, and the benefit cut raises the necessary wage. If union wage negotiations are affected by this change on the supply side, then the net wage rises. At any x^* this causes the demand curve, L^D, to shift to the left (see figure 3.5). Unemployment falls, but as far as employment in the market sector is concerned, we have two conflicting forces. The benefit cut reduces queue unemployment, pushing down the equilibrium

x^*, but also discourages employment in the market sector through the rise in the $w(1 - t)/x^*$ ratio. In the case of figure 3.5 the former effect dominates, leaving the overall conclusion unchanged, but it shows the relevance of general equilibrium considerations.

That the union wage differential would be increased by cuts in benefits is a logical consequence of the benefit subsidizing the job queue, but this conclusion may be changed if the level of benefit enters the wage bargain directly. Suppose benefits spill over to those in self-employment, as considered briefly in the case of home production in section 3.2. In that case, the relevant expression in equation (3.21) becomes $(x^* + b)$ rather than x^*; and the cut in benefit reduces the bargained wage at any level of (U/V). On the other hand, the benefit no longer serves to induce people to enter the queue for a market job. An alternative assumption is that the transfer is confined to those who have previously been employed in the union sector, and therefore constitutes part of the "social wage," or remuneration "package." A cut in benefits in these circumstances may lead unions to demand compensating increases in money wages, the reverse of the previous prediction.

These two examples underline the need to consider more fully the fine structure of unemployment benefit—the conditions under which it is paid—and this is investigated in the next chapter. Definite conclusions should be postponed.

3.6   In Lieu of a Conclusion

From the labor market model considered in this chapter, it should be apparent that the impact of scaling back unemployment benefit is less straightforward than commonly supposed. There is a tendency to focus on the obvious incentive issue—shortening the job queue—without taking account of the general equilibrium impact on the attractiveness of employment covered by unemployment insurance. Similarly, the consequences of benefit cuts may depend sensitively on the conditions of entitlement.

There are indeed several reasons why any conclusion should be treated as preliminary, not least that the model of unemployment embodies only one of the many explanations of unemployment. As we saw earlier, there are a variety of (possibly complementary) theories, and we need to consider the implications of alternatives. A second problem is that the model does not allow for differentiation within the labor force and the possible impact of benefits on wage differentials. Both of these objections are addressed in the next chapter, where I describe a model of sectoral wage differentials in a segmented labor market, where wage rigidities arise on account of efficiency wages as well as union wage bargaining.

4   Unemployment Insurance in a Segmented Labor Market

Unemployment benefit in chapter 3 was treated simply as the income received by those not in work or self-employment. In this respect, the analysis parallelled much of the economic literature on unemployment benefit, which assumes that the benefit operates just like a wage for the unemployed: for example, "the wage when working is w, and is b when not working" (Oswald 1986, p. 369). Yet in reality this is not the case. In the first section of this chapter, I consider some of the important attributes of unemployment insurance and assistance. In section 4.2 I seek to provide a richer treatment of the labor market, allowing for segmentation and differential flows between the primary and secondary sectors of the economy. This model is used in section 4.3 to examine the impact of cuts in unemployment benefit, taking account of its institutional structure. Section 4.4 is concerned with alternatives to unemployment benefit.

4.1   Real-World Unemployment Insurance

The typical economics treatment of unemployment benefit assumes, as far as the recipient is concerned, that

1. there are no contribution conditions related to past employment,

2. the benefit is paid irrespective of the reasons for entry into unemployment,

3. the benefit is paid independently of the recipient's efforts to search for new work, or of availability for work,

4. there is no penalty for the refusal of job offers,

5. the benefit is paid for an unlimited duration,

6. neither eligibility for benefit nor the amount of benefit are affected by the level of income of other household members.

On this basis, all of those out of work are assumed to be in receipt of unemployment compensation. However, as noted in chapter 2, real-world benefits do not satisfy these assumptions.

In table 4.1 are summarized some of the main institutional details that relate to eligibility for unemployment insurance in the fifteen European Union countries at mid-1995, based on the European Community's MISSOC (Mutual Information System on Social Protection in the Community).[13] Real-world unemployment insurance is subject first of all to contribution conditions. In order to receive benefit, people must typically have contributed a minimum amount over their working life, and often there is an additional condition regarding *recent* insured employment. In Germany, for instance, a person has to have had at least 12 months of employment under insurance cover during the previous 3 years. In Finland there has to have been at least 26 weeks of employment during the last 24 months, or, for the self-employed, 24 months of business activity during the last 48 months. People may also be ineligible if they have entered unemployment voluntarily or as a result of industrial misconduct. This is the second important institutional feature of many unemployment insurance schemes. For example, in France there is a requirement not to have left previous employment voluntarily without good cause. In the United States, not shown, people may be disqualified from unemployment insurance for voluntary separation without good cause or discharge for misconduct. In the United Kingdom the maximum period of disqualification from benefit for loss of job without just cause or industrial misconduct was extended from 6 weeks to 13 weeks in 1986, and then to 26 weeks in 1988. Under the jobseeker's allowance, which replaced unemployment benefit in October 1996, a person disqualified for the maximum period loses *all* entitlement to social insurance.

The third condition for receipt of unemployment insurance is that of being available for and seeking work. In Spain claimants are required to be able and willing to work and to be at the disposal of the employment office. In many cases benefit receipt is tied to registration at the unemployment or employment office. Fourthly, failure to accept employment if offered is ground for terminating benefit: for example, in the Netherlands a condition is that a person should not have refused suitable employment. In the United Kingdom the monitoring of the unemployed has been increased over time, particularly since 1979 (see Atkinson and Micklewright 1989).

Finally, while unemployment insurance is typically determined on an individual basis, so that assumption (6) is satisfied, in all cases except Belgium there is a limited duration to unemployment *insurance*. For example, the United Kingdom now limits the insurance-linked jobseeker's allowance to 6 months (it was 1 year in 1995). This is of course different from the unlimited durations taken in the empirical analysis of Layard, Nickell, and Jackman (1991), described above in chapter 2. They, however, took both unemployment insurance and unemployment assistance or general social assistance. People

Table 4.1
Unemployment insurance in European Union, 1995

Country (date of first law)	Contribution conditions	Conditions for continued receipt	Duration
Belgium (1924)	Vary with age from 312 days of work in previous 18 months and 624 in previous 36 months	To be without work and without earnings; to be fit for work; registered for employment	No limit (except for certain cases of longterm unemployment)
Denmark (1907) Optional insurance funds	1 year of insurance with fund, and minimum of 26 weeks of insured employment in 3 preceding years	To be unemployed involuntarily; to search actively for employment; signed on at employment office	3 years (4 years for initial period)
Germany (1927)	At least 12 months of insured employment in 3 preceding years	To be available for work; registered at employment exchange	6 months to 1 year for those aged under 42
Greece (1954)	125 days of work in preceding 14 months, or 200 days (80 days for first time claimants) in preceding 2 years	To be unemployed involuntarily; to be fit for work; registered at employment exchange and at the disposal of the exchange	5 months to 1 year
Spain (1961)	12 months contributions in preceding 6 years	To have lost previous job involuntarily; to be able and willing to work; to be at the disposal of the employment office	Varies

France (1940)	4 months insurance in previous 8 months	Not to have left previous employment voluntarily without good cause; to be looking for work and physically able to work; registered for work	4 months to 5 years
Ireland (1911)	39 weeks contributions paid, and 39 weeks paid or credited in preceding contribution year	To be free from disqualification; to be fit for work; available for and seeking work; registered as unemployed	15 months
Italy (1919)	2 years insurance, and 52 weeks contributions in previous 2 years	Registered at unemployment agency	180 days
Luxembourg (1921)	26 weeks of employment in previous year	To be involuntarily unemployed; to be fit for work; available for work; registered for employment and accept suitable employment offered	1 year
Netherlands (1986)	26 weeks of paid employment in previous 39 months	To be capable of and available for work; registered at employment exchange; not to have refused suitable employment	6 months–5 years
Austria (1920)	52 weeks insurance in previous 2 years	To be capable of work and willing to work	20 weeks–52 weeks

Table 4.1 (continued)

Country (date of first law)	Contribution conditions	Conditions for continued receipt	Duration
Portugal (1975)	540 days of insured employment (or assimilated situation) in previous 2 years	To be capable of and available for work; registered at employment office	10 months–30 months
Finland (1917)	26 weeks of employment in previous 2 years (self-employed also covered)	To be capable of and available for work; looking for full-time work; registered at employment office	100 weeks
Sweden (1934) Optional insurance funds	1 year insurance, and at least 80 days of work (or equivalent) over 5 months	To be unemployed involuntarily; to be fit for work and not prevented from taking suitable work; registered at employment office	60 weeks aged under 55
United Kingdom (1911)	Minimum insured employment in 1 of 2 relevant contribution years, and minimum contributions paid or credited in both years	To be unemployed involuntarily; to be capable of and available for work; to be actively searching for employment; claimed benefit	1 year

Source: European Commission 1996.

may qualify for assistance on the expiry of unemployment insurance. In Germany *Arbeitslosenhilfe* may be payable on the exhaustion of *Arbeitslosengeld*; in the United Kingdom income support may (in 1995) have been available to those who had exhausted entitlement to the insurance benefit.

Unemployment *assistance* is closer to the hypothetical "wage when not working" in that there may be no contribution conditions, and that it may be paid for an unlimited duration. However, the assumptions (2), (3), and (4) are not typically valid. People may be disqualified from unemployment assistance in the case of voluntary quitting or dismissal for industrial misconduct; and benefit may be withdrawn if claimants are not considered to be actively seeking employment or refuse suitable job offers. Moreover, unemployment assistance has the further attributes that eligibility depends, via a means test, on 1) other income and assets, and 2) the income and assets of other household members. Unemployed people may find that when their insurance benefits expire there is no entitlement to assistance because they have savings in the bank. An unemployed man whose wife is in paid work may find that her earnings take them over the means-test limit, so that he receives no further assistance when his insurance benefit ends.

These institutional features have to be incorporated into the theoretical analysis (as has been emphasized in Atkinson and Micklewright 1991 and Atkinson 1992a). Undoubtedly the rules are applied imperfectly. Not all those who are ineligible are disqualified from benefit. But it seems to me perverse to ignore the conditions under which benefits are paid, since the conditions are designed to meet the objection most commonly leveled against unemployment benefits by economists: that they discourage return to work. Conditions on work-seeking have been an essential part of the history of unemployment benefit (see King 1995). Most governments allocate significant resources to enforcement, and for benefit recipients the conditions are a very real part of their lives. Whereas most economic models of unemployment benefit assume that the conditions are completely ineffective, it seems to me more reasonable to assume as a first approximation that the conditions apply. The conditions are certainly very real to many claimants.[14]

In what follows, I consider a general form of unemployment benefit that has the following features:

1'. there are contribution conditions related to past employment so that a person must have worked for a period H in order to qualify for benefit,

2'. benefit is refused where the claimant has quit voluntarily or has been dismissed for industrial misconduct,

3'. receipt of benefit is conditional on the recipient making demonstrable efforts to search for new employment, and on being available for employment,

4'. receipt of benefit is conditional on the recipient accepting suitable job offers,

5'. there is a probability that benefit may be terminated, as where insurance benefit ends and there is no entitlement to unemployment assistance.

An important implication of these institutional features is that people may be unemployed and not receive unemployment benefit (neither insurance nor assistance). They may be disqualified from the outset, or in the course of receipt, or they may exhaust entitlement. We need therefore to distinguish between unemployment with and without benefit, the value of these two states being denoted by Ω_b and Ω_u. The number of unemployed with benefit is denoted by U_b and the number without benefit by U_u. The total number of unemployed, $U_b + U_u$, is denoted by U.

Empirically, nonreceipt of benefit is important. In the United States, McMurrer and Chasanov find that unemployment insurance claimants were about 30% of total unemployment in the early 1990s, and that over the postwar period "the percentage of the unemployed who receive Unemployment Insurance benefits has declined steadily, with a particularly sharp decline in the early 1980s" (1995, p. 38). The reasons for the decline are in part legislative changes, but they also include demographic shifts and the decline of the unionized manufacturing sector (Blank and Card 1991). This points to the need to consider unemployment benefit within an economic model that allows for sectoral differentiation. The rolling back of the welfare state may be happening endogenously as "good" jobs covered by unemployment benefits are replaced by "bad" jobs that have no such coverage. The same conclusion follows from the Continental discussion of social transfers as a source of exclusion, where the conditions of social insurance and other benefits limit them to a privileged class of workers. In France and other countries, the welfare state has been criticized from the left of the political spectrum on the grounds that contribution and other conditions are to the advantage of those in the better paid, unionized sector of the economy. I therefore turn to a segmented labor market model.

4.2   A Segmented Labor Market

The segmented labor market model outlined here follows the tradition originated by Doeringer and Piore (1971) and developed by, among others, Bulow and Summers (1986) and McDonald and Solow (1985). There is a primary sector in which L_p workers are employed each earning a wage w_p, and a secondary sector in which L_s workers are employed each earning a wage w_s. Both sectors produce the same output, whose price is taken as the numeraire. The total potential labor force is fixed at N.

As already signaled, the model allows for a further element in the explanation of unemployment: the existence of efficiency wages such that in equilibrium a firm finds it profitable to pay a higher wage than that which clears the market. Efficiency wages may take a number of forms (Akerlof and Yellen 1986). Firms pay wage premia to reduce turnover or to attract higher quality workers; alternatively, there is the partial gift exchange theory of Akerlof (1982 and 1984), where employers who pay a wage premium raise group work norms. Here I take the shirking version of the efficiency wage hypothesis advanced by Shapiro and Stiglitz (1984), among others. Workers are not monitored continuously and are induced to supply effort by the payment of an efficiency wage premium that is lost if they are fired.

In earlier work (Atkinson 1992a) examining the impact of unemployment insurance, I have used such a segmented labor market model, with, as in Bulow and Summers (1986), efficiency wages being paid in the primary sector. There are, however, two reasons why this treatment now seems to me unsatisfactory. The first is that efficiency wages on their own do not account for the existence of unemployment in a two sector model if employment is always possible in the secondary sector (the original Shapiro and Stiglitz model is of a one sector economy). Unemployment only arises on account of the queue for jobs in the primary sector. The second is that potential shirking seems more applicable to the secondary than to the primary sector of the economy. A situation where workers have to be induced to put in effort by the threat of dismissal is more likely to be found in the fast-food industry than in BMW or Zeneca. In the model that follows, shirking-based efficiency wages are assumed to apply in the secondary sector, whereas wages in the primary sector are governed, as in McDonald and Solow (1985), by union/employer bargaining of the kind discussed in chapter 3.

In both sectors there is a risk that jobs will be involuntarily terminated. The probability in the primary sector is denoted by δ_p and that in the secondary sector by δ_s. It is, however, a standard assumption about a segmented labor market that jobs are more secure in the primary sector, and it is assumed that δ_p is substantially smaller than δ_s. These probabilities affect entitlement to unemployment insurance in that the survival probability at the point where benefit entitlement commences, H, is $e^{-\delta H}$. For simplicity, I assume that δ_p is sufficiently small that we can take all primary sector workers as qualifying for benefit. The probability of secondary sector workers being entitled to benefit on involuntary job loss is written as v, where this may incorporate elements of discrimination against secondary sector workers as well as lower probability of survival in employment.

Primary Sector

In the primary sector it is assumed that, as in chapter 3, wages are determined by trade union bargaining, and employment by the demand function

$$L_p^D = Cw_p^{-1/\beta}, \tag{4.1}$$

where C is a constant. Employers and unions maximize

$$\Pi^\zeta \{L_p^D(\Omega_p - \Omega_s)\}, \tag{4.2}$$

where ζ is a positive parameter measuring the relative bargaining power of the employers (now assumed to be constant, rather than depending on labor market conditions), and where the union maximizes the difference in total expected present value from the employment of L workers at wage w_p, compared with their being employed in the secondary sector. The first-order condition (3.19) may be rewritten

$$(\Omega_p - \Omega_s)[1/\beta + \zeta(1 - \beta)/\beta] = w_p \partial [\Omega_p - \Omega_s]/\partial w_p, \qquad (4.3)$$

where β is the share of profits. Neither employers nor unions offer unemployment benefits.

Primary sector vacancies are filled from the unemployed who are assumed to stand an equal chance of receiving a job offer whether or not they receive benefit. (There is assumed to be no recruitment directly from secondary sector employment.) The likelihood of getting a job in the primary sector depends on the effectiveness of matching, as in the previous chapter, but I make the simpler assumption here that, with a total of U unemployed workers and V vacancies, the instantaneous probability of a job offer is the ratio of V to U. A primary sector job is always accepted by an unemployed worker, so that the transition rate to primary sector jobs is V/U, denoted by μ_p. At any time, the number of job terminations in the primary sector is $\delta_p L_p$, and in equilibrium this is equal to the number of vacancies, so that

$$\mu_p = V/U = \delta_p L_p/U. \qquad (4.4)$$

Workers are assumed to evaluate alternatives in terms solely of the expected present value of a continuous stream of returns, discounted at a constant rate r over an infinite horizon. The present value of a job in the primary sector, Ω_p, is given by, in a stationary situation,

$$r\Omega_p = w_p(1 - t) - \varepsilon - \delta_p(\Omega_p - \Omega_b). \tag{4.5}$$

This is the same as equation (3.15), allowing for the social security tax at rate t on wages, for the cost of effort (ε), discussed below, and for the fact that unemployment is insured (the present value of the state of unemployment benefit recipient is denoted by Ω_b).

Secondary Sector

It is in the secondary sector that we assume the existence of an efficiency wage. As in the model of Shapiro and Stiglitz (1984), a worker can choose between supplying effort, at cost ε, and the alternative of not putting in effort and facing a risk λ of being monitored, in which case the worker is fired. "Effort" is assumed here, following Bulow and Summers (1986), to involve the loss of personal services, which have then to be purchased in the form of output. Both ε and λ are assumed constant over time. Firms find it profitable to pay a wage premium such that a worker is indifferent between putting in effort and shirking. (See MacLeod and Malcomson 1993 for discussion of the nature of the contract.)

In the model of Shapiro and Stiglitz (1984), it is assumed that a worker sacked for shirking receives unemployment benefit. However, this ignores the institutional features outlined in the previous section. Dismissal for shirking is an example of industrial misconduct, and is likely to lead to disqualification from benefit. This means that the wage premium has to be such that

$$\varepsilon = \lambda[\Omega_s - \Omega_u], \tag{4.6}$$

where Ω_s denotes the expected present value of holding a secondary sector job and Ω_u denotes the expected present value of being unemployed without benefit. Unemployment benefit does not enter directly into the "no shirking condition."

The present value of a job in the secondary sector held by a worker who is induced by (4.6) to supply effort ε is given by

$$r\Omega_s = w_s(1 - t) - \varepsilon - \delta_s[\Omega_s - v\Omega_b - (1 - v)\Omega_u], \tag{4.7}$$

where Ω_u is the present value associated with the state of unemployment without benefit. It is assumed that the secondary sector recruits from the unemployed in the same way as the primary sector: the instantaneous probability of a secondary sector job offer to an unemployed person, denoted by μ_s, is equal to the ratio of vacancies, $\delta_s L_s$, to the total number of unemployed. The demand for workers is assumed to be

$$L_s^D\{w_s\} \text{ where } L_s^{D\prime} \leq 0. \tag{4.8}$$

Unemployment

The conditions on benefit receipt affect the length of time for which it is received. Recipients face two risks. The first is that insurance benefit expires and they are not eligible for assistance (for example, because they have a partner in employment). The second is that benefit is terminated on the grounds that they are not actively seeking work or are not available for work. These two considerations are represented schematically in the model by assuming that those in receipt of insurance benefit face a probability γ that benefit expires. In stationary equilibrium the valuation placed on the state of insured unemployment is therefore

$$r\Omega_b = b + \mu_p[\Omega_p - \Omega_b] + \mu_s[\Omega_s - \Omega_b] - \gamma[\Omega_b - \Omega_u]. \tag{4.9}$$

It may be noted that I am assuming a flat-rate benefit. If b were related to past earnings, then we would have to distinguish

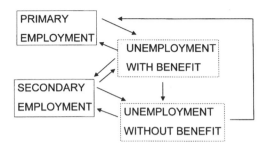

Figure 4.1
Labor market flows

between those unemployed who previously held primary sector jobs and those who previously held secondary sector jobs.

Finally, the valuation placed on the state of unemployment without benefit must satisfy

$$r\Omega_u = \mu_p[\Omega_p - \Omega_u] + \mu_s[\Omega_s - \Omega_u]. \tag{4.10}$$

The possible labor market flows are summarized in figure 4.1. For an equilibrium state, inflows must balance outflows, which requires that

$$\mu_p(U_b + U_u) = \delta_p L_p \quad \text{(which is equation (4.4) above)},$$
$$\tag{4.11a}$$

$$\mu_s(U_b + U_u) = \delta_s L_s, \tag{4.11b}$$

$$\delta_p L_p + v\delta_s L_s = (\gamma + \mu_p + \mu_s)U_b, \tag{4.11c}$$

$$\gamma U_b + (1 - v)\delta_s L_s = (\mu_p + \mu_s)U_u. \tag{4.11d}$$

The final condition is that

$$L_p + L_s + U = N. \tag{4.11e}$$

The determination of the labor market equilibrium in this model can be sketched as follows. (I do not attempt to provide a full solution here.) I focus on the equilibrium state, although in a fuller analysis we should treat explicitly the process of adjustment, as for example in the work of Pissarides (1985, 1990) and Mortensen (1989). This involves introducing the change in "asset" values, Ω, whereas the capital gains or losses in the value of different states have been set to zero in the earlier equations.

One important part of the solution is indeed the block of equations (4.5), (4.7), (4.9), and (4.10) determining the valuations Ω_p, Ω_s, Ω_b, and Ω_u, as linear functions of w_p, w_s, and b, where the coefficients include μ_p and μ_s, which are endogenous (depending on levels of employment and unemployment). For example (leaving aside additional terms in ε):

$$\Omega_p \sim w_p(1-t)[1/(r+\delta_p) - \delta_s\mu_s/R]$$

$$+ w_s(1-t)\delta_p\mu_s/R + \delta_p b/(r+\gamma+\mu_p+\mu_s)$$

$$\times [1/(r+\delta_p) - (1-v)\delta_s\mu_s/R] \qquad (4.12a)$$

and

$$\Omega_s \sim w_p(1-t)\delta_s\mu_p/R + w_s(1-t)$$

$$\times [1/(r+\delta_s) - \delta_p\mu_p/R] + \delta_s b/(r+\gamma+\mu_p+\mu_s)$$

$$\times [v/(r+\delta_s) + (1-v)\delta_p\mu_p/R], \qquad (4.12b)$$

where

$$R \equiv (r+\delta_p)(r+\delta_s)(r+\mu_p+\mu_s). \qquad (4.12c)$$

If, for example, a primary sector job were simply held at risk δ_p, and the work career ended with the job, then we would have the first term in (4.12a). The present value, however, also depends on w_s, since the person may lose the primary sector job and enter the secondary sector. And while unemployed they receive benefit, which is discounted by an amount that takes account of the exit probabilities. The value placed on unemployment benefit is an increasing function of δ_p, the risk of job termination. For a person in the secondary sector, w_p enters the valuation for the same reason, via the probability of losing the secondary sector job and then of finding one in the primary sector. For the person laid off by Joe's Cafe it may be the best thing that happened to him if he is subsequently taken on by a firm of catering consultants. The benefit level enters the valuation of a secondary sector job, even where $v = 0$, since the person may lose the secondary sector job, enter the primary sector, and then become unemployed (with insurance) again.

The valuations of the different states have to satisfy the conditions on the determination of wages in the two sectors: equations (4.3) and (4.6). We can solve these equations for w_p and w_s as functions of the parameters and b. These then determine L_p and L_s from equations (4.1) and (4.8). In order for there to be an equilibrium, these have to be consistent with the values of μ_p and μ_s in equations (4.11). A positive relation between the reemployment probabilities, μ_p and μ_s, and the wage rates means that L_p and L_s are declining functions of these probabilities, so that we can see from (4.11a) and (4.11b) how an equilibrium can be constructed.

The underlying economics may be seen from figure 4.2, which shows the relation between w_p and w_s. Looking first at the "no shirking condition" (NSC), which depends on the difference between Ω_s and Ω_u, we see that the former depends on w_s, obviously, but also on b via the probability δ_s of job termination multiplied by the probability v of benefit coverage, and on w_p. Ω_u also depends on w_p, w_s, and b, but indirectly via the probabilities of getting a job (for example, w_p is multiplied by μ_p). The difference $(\Omega_s - \Omega_u)$ is therefore an increasing func-

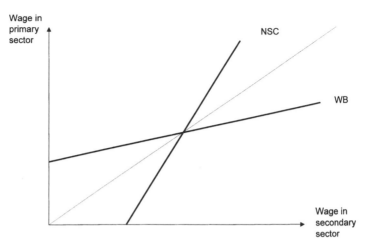

Figure 4.2
No shirking condition and wage bargain lines

tion of w_s; on the other hand it decreases with w_p, since given the assumption that the primary sector does not recruit from those currently working in the secondary sector, an unemployed person is "nearer" to a primary sector job. (The realism of this assumption can be debated.) The resulting NSC line is shown in figure 4.2. It slopes up, since a rise in w_p means that secondary sector employers have to pay a higher premium to induce effort. Where the recruitment link between the primary sector and unemployment is weak, the slope is high. The location of the intercept on the horizontal axis depends on, among other parameters, the cost of effort, ε, the probability of being monitored, λ, and on the level of benefit (which enters the NSC indirectly through its effect on both Ω_s and Ω_u).

The difference between the value of a primary sector job and a secondary sector job, Ω_p and Ω_s, which enters the trade union/employer wage bargain (WB), is an increasing function of w_p and a decreasing function of w_s. This gives rise to the line marked WB in figure 4.2. It is also a function of the level of benefit, as discussed below, but in the absence of benefits the intercept of the WB curve with the vertical axis is above the origin. The WB line is steeper the larger the union mark-up, which, as noted in chapter 3, increases as the share of capital increases and the relative strength of employers decreases; the slope is less steep the larger the difference between δ_p and δ_s. The case shown in figure 4.2 corresponds to that where union bargaining strength is sufficiently moderate, or the differential in job security sufficiently large, that the slope of the WB line is less than that of the NSC, and there is an intersection as shown.

At such an equilibrium unemployment arises, not just because people are queuing for primary sector (union) jobs but also because the efficiency wage sets a floor to wages in the secondary sector. In equilibrium there is a wage differential between the two sectors, shown in figure 4.2 by the dotted line. This wage differential clearly depends on the relative bargaining power of unions and employers, but also on the conditions of employment in the two sectors. Any narrowing that may have arisen in recent years as a result of curbs on union power, notably in the United Kingdom, could well have been offset by moves to a more flexible labor market, causing jobs in the primary sector to be more precarious. As Bertola and Ichino (1995) have argued, increased volatility of employment may lead to widening wage dispersion.

4.3   Impact of Cuts in Unemployment Benefit

The model set out in the previous section provides a rich framework for the analysis of the impact of policy changes. For instance, the impact of a reduction in the payroll tax may be seen from figure 4.2. A rise in $(1 - t)$ reduces the intercepts of the NSC and WB lines, and hence, in the case shown, lowers the wage rates at any given reemployment probabilities, μ_p and μ_s, and increases the level of employment. As noted by Pissarides (1998), the consequences of cuts in employment taxes depend on the assumption made about benefit determination. The above statement referred to the case where the level of benefit is held constant; where the replacement rate is held constant as a proportion of net wages, the impact on employment is attenuated.

Here I concentrate primarily on the effect of reducing the level or coverage of unemployment benefits, and the alternatives to those benefits, taking the tax rate as given. What are the consequences of a reduction in benefit levels or in benefit coverage? The effect on wages can be understood in terms of the relation between the coverage parameter, v, for secondary sector workers, and other parameters. Suppose that

$$1/[1 + (r + \delta_p)/\mu_p] < v(\delta_s/\delta_p)$$

$$< 1 + (\delta_s - \delta_p)/[r + \mu_p + \mu_s + \delta_p]. \tag{4.13}$$

The central term is the relative chance in the two sectors that a job will be terminated and benefit received. This "benefit relevance" parameter depends both on the extent of coverage (v) and on the risk of employment termination. A useful benchmark is the case where this is equal to one: that is, where the higher risk of job termination in secondary employment is exactly offset by the lower rate of eligibility for benefit. It may be noted that if the right hand inequality holds, then a primary sector worker values unemployment benefit more highly than a secondary sector worker.

Where condition (4.13) holds, a cut in benefit level, b, shifts the NSC and WB curves as shown in figure 4.3. Secondary

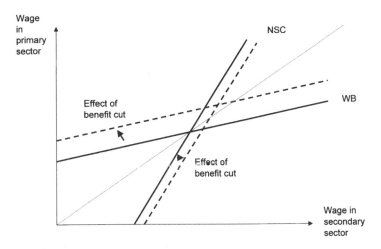

Figure 4.3
First-round effect of cut in unemployment benefit level

sector employers have to pay a higher premium, since part of the benefit to the job is being reduced. In the wage bargain, unemployment benefit is relatively advantageous to the primary sector, so that a benefit cut leads unions to seek a larger wage differential. In these circumstances, the cut in benefits leads to a rise in the wage rates at any given reemployment probabilities, μ_p and μ_s, and hence reduces the level of employment. (Figure 4.3 shows the "first-round" effect in that it does not allow for the consequential adjustments in the reemployment probabilities.) Where the benefit relevance parameter is close to the lower limit in (4.13), then the wage differential widens, as shown in figure 4.3. Benefit cuts lead to greater wage dispersion.

Benefits may be curtailed not just through reductions in benefit levels but also through shorter durations and tightened administration. These are represented here by the parameter γ, which is the probability of benefit termination. A rise in γ has the same effect as a fall in b, shifting the intercepts in the same direction.

In contrast to what is typically supposed in the economic literature, unemployment benefits, as such, may favor employment, as shown in a different model in Atkinson (1992a). It does not necessarily follow that reductions in the social wage lead to rises in wages and hence falls in employment. Where the condition (4.13) does not hold, then the NSC line shifts to the left or the WB line shifts down. However, the important point is that unemployment benefit does not operate in the way typically assumed. The predictions may be contrasted with those others have reached in efficiency wage models. Stiglitz, for example, has summarized the conclusions drawn from the shirking model that he constructed with Shapiro (Shapiro and Stiglitz 1984):

Consider, for instance, an increase in the unemployment compensation. In the 'shirking' version of the efficiency wage model, this results in firms having to raise their wages in order to induce workers not to shirk (the penalty for being caught is smaller at any fixed wage and unemployed level). This in turn results in a higher equilibrium unemployment rate and a higher real wage. (Stiglitz 1986, p. 188)

Their conclusion is different from that reached here because they assume that workers who are dismissed for shirking receive unemployment benefit, whereas in reality they face the risk of disqualification. Similarly, in their *Handbook of Labor Economics* article, Johnson and Layard consider, among other models, one in which firms are concerned about the rate at which workers quit, this depending on the ratio of the wage offered to the expected income on quitting, which in turn depends on the replacement rate offered by the unemployment benefit system. There is a cost-minimizing level of quitting, which determines the equilibrium relation between the replacement rate and the level of unemployment: "If the replacement rate is higher, quitting becomes more attractive and, to offset this, unemployment has to be higher" (Johnson and Layard 1986, p. 961). This finding again depends on the assumption that workers who quit their jobs voluntarily are eligible for unemployment insurance. In our model, where we have allowed for the institutional features of unemployment insurance, the impact of benefits (holding taxes constant) is the reverse of that found in these studies.

I should stress that the finding that a cut in unemployment benefit may *increase* unemployment is not new. The same conclusion was reached, for instance, by Axell and Lang (1990), but the mechanism is different. In their case, firms decide to offer fewer high-wage jobs in a model of search in both labor and product markets (see Albrecht, Axell, and Lang 1986). The difference is that I have focused here on the institutional features of the benefit system.

Alternatives

We have modeled above a typical form of unemployment benefit; consideration is now given to two alternative forms of benefit. The first is a benefit limited to the primary sector, as might arise if unemployment benefits were provided solely via collective bargaining.[15]

Where secondary sector workers are not entitled to benefits ($v = 0$), benefits become essentially part of the primary sector remuneration package. In the union negotiations they therefore play a more powerful role, reducing the wage demanded by the actuarial value of the benefit, which is the risk of job termination times the benefit discounted at a rate r plus the

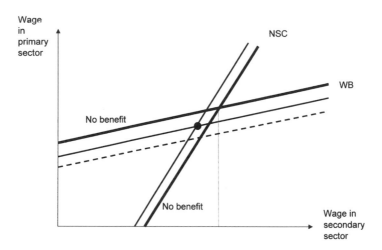

Figure 4.4
Alternatives to current unemployment benefit

risk of exit, where exit may be to employment $(\mu_p + \mu_s)$ or to benefit loss (ε). Compared with a no benefit situation, the primary wage is reduced by this amount (see dashed line in figure 4.4), and the secondary wage is unaffected. Compared with a situation where benefits are paid to secondary workers such that (4.13) is satisfied, as indicated by the dot in figure 4.4, the secondary wage would be higher at any given reemployment probabilities and hence employment lower.

The situation where unemployment benefits follow the segmentation of the labor market has been examined by Disney (1982), drawing on and criticizing Marxist analyses. As he notes, one can seek to explain in this way the differential development of unemployment insurance and social assistance, the latter means-tested scheme being that most applicable to the more disadvantaged workers: "the heterogeneity of insurance treatment reflects the heterogeneity of the labour market" (Disney 1982, p. 45).

Reform in the opposite direction from that described above would be to make benefits universal. Suppose that unemployment insurance and assistance were to be replaced by a citizen's income, payable unconditionally at rate i to everyone. Such a benefit would add i/r to the present value of each labor market state, and would thus be neutral with regard to both the no shirking condition and the wage bargain. The "no benefit" solution in figure 4.4 is therefore the same as that with a citizen's income. In the case shown, the introduction of the citizen's income would cause wages to rise compared to a benefit of the current type satisfying (4.13). In the secondary sector employers would have to pay a larger wage premium, since there would be no disqualification from benefit in the event of dismissal. In the primary sector the advantage to unionized workers in terms of social insurance would be lost.

4.4 Conclusion

In this chapter, I have focused on the impact of unemployment benefits on the level of employment, arguing that cutting benefits as such may—contrary to the general presumption—have adverse consequences. It should be noted that this is different from arguments, made for example by Diamond (1981), that unemployment compensation is welfare-improving. Here I am concerned not with welfare, or distortions, but with the impact on the quantity of employment. The statement also refers to the specific effect of benefits, rather than the taxes necessary to finance them. Cuts in payroll taxes increase employment in the model studied, and this should form part of the overall assessment, but it is important to identify the different elements in the argument. The key to the results described here is the interaction between the institutional structure of unemployment benefit and labor market behavior in the form of efficiency wages and union/employer wage bargaining. The conditions under which benefits are paid, and the coverage of benefits, are crucial in understanding their impact. Institutional features are too important to leave to the footnotes.

5   Public Choice and Unemployment Insurance

The calls to roll back the welfare state are themselves a proper subject for analysis, so I turn now to this question of "political economy." We need to understand not just the economic consequences of particular measures—such as a scaling back of unemployment insurance—but also the reasons that lie behind such policies, since they are in part at least endogenous. If we do not understand the reasons why people are calling for a scaling back of transfers, then we may be surprised if the enactment of such a policy sets in train further political reactions. These may either generate a cumulative decline, going far beyond the initial proposals, or else initiate a cycle of policy reversals.

Issues of political economy are well illustrated by unemployment insurance, which has typically been among the most politically sensitive parts of the welfare state. I begin with a brief, and oversimplified, account of legislative history, with particular reference to recent developments. I then consider some of the explanations that have been advanced.

5.1   Changes in Unemployment Insurance

Both unemployment itself and unemployment benefits have been highly political subjects in most countries. Legislation in this field has often been difficult and controversial. Although in many countries there have long been (limited) provisions for helping the unemployed under social assistance schemes (poor law relief), formal unemployment benefits of an insurance type came relatively late (see the dates of the first laws listed in table 4.1).

Once enacted, unemployment insurance schemes have been subject to hostile forces when they have been called on to deliver the promised income protection. The situation in Germany in the early 1930s (public insurance was introduced in 1927) has been described by Schmid, Reissert, and Bruche:

The system was unable to cope with its first test, the depression of the early 1930s. It had already come under pressure by the end of the 1920s as a result of increasing deficits, which ... were an occasion for constant changes: increases in contributions, exclusion from coverage, reductions in the level and duration of benefits, and finally even a means test (incompatible with insurance principles).... At the end of the Weimar Republic only 11 percent of the unemployed were receiving benefits. (1992, p. 73)

Anglo-Saxon Experience

Has the unemployment of the latter part of the twentieth century led to a similar reaction? In the United Kingdom the response to rising unemployment in the 1980s was very similar to that just described in the Weimar Republic. When unemployment rose in the 1980s to record postwar levels, the reaction was to restrict benefit generosity and entitlement. As already noted in chapter 2, the replacement rate, already low by European standards, was significantly reduced. The fall between 1981 and 1991 is shown in figure 5.1, which is based on OECD calculations for eleven European countries and the United States. The replacement rate is a summary measure of benefit entitlements, based on an average for eighteen cases:

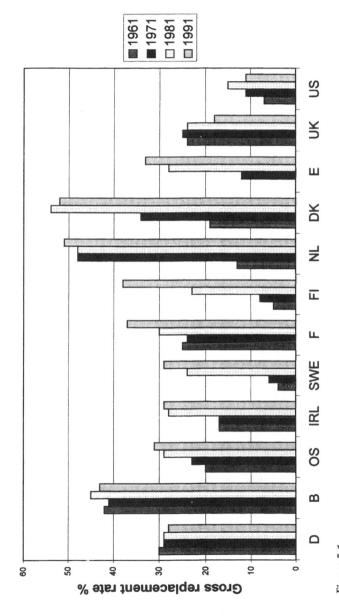

Figure 5.1
Replacement Rates, 1961–1991. Source: OECD 1994, table 8.B.1.

crossing three family situations by three unemployment durations by two earnings levels.

In the period 1979–88 the United Kingdom government made no fewer than seventeen significant changes to National Insurance unemployment benefit (Atkinson and Micklewright 1989). Of these, two changes were favorable to the unemployed (one in response to a European Community directive on equal treatment of men and women). Some changes may have been either positive or negative in their impact. But the great majority represented

• a reduction in the level of benefits (for example, the abolition of the earnings related supplement, which means that there is now no relation with past earnings, or the abolition of child additions for claimants with children),

• reduced coverage of benefits (for example, tightening of contribution conditions and abolition of lower rate benefits for those not meeting full contribution conditions),

• tighter administration (for example, more stringent availability for work test or extension of disqualification period from 6 weeks to 26 weeks).

Overall, the measures taken in the United Kingdom since 1979 have seriously reduced the coverage and generosity of unemployment benefit. For example, in the two years after the introduction of the Stricter Benefit Regime the number of claimants sanctioned is reported to have nearly tripled (Murray 1996). Indeed, unemployment insurance as such has now been abolished and replaced (from October 1996) by a new jobseeker's allowance, paid for a maximum of six months on the basis of contributions and thereafter subject to income and assets tests applied to the claimant and partner. It was estimated that the measure would save some £210 million a year (around 10 percent of total spending) and that some 165,000 would lose entitlement (around a tenth), of whom 70,000 would not qualify for means-tested assistance (Finn 1996).

In the United States a range of measures were taken in the 1980s by the federal government to reduce the value and coverage of unemployment benefit. These included the taxation of benefits, partially from 1979 and fully from 1986, and the requirement that states repay with interest federal loans to their trust funds, which caused states in turn to tighten eligibility to unemployment insurance and to reduce benefits. The Federal General Accounting Office reported that, between 1981 and 1987, no fewer than fourty-four states adopted tighter eligibility standards or stricter disqualification provisions (McMurrer and Chasanov 1995, p. 35).

Continental Europe

The position in Continental Europe is different. The standard account of the postwar period is one of expanding unemployment benefit provisions. According to Siebert (1997): "The rise of the European welfare state in the 1970s effectively raised the reservation wage by a whole set of measures: the duration of benefits was often increased; it was made easier to obtain unemployment benefits" (p. 50). He goes on to say that these countries have not followed the Anglo-Saxon route in recent years: "The majority of European countries have made only marginal changes to their labor market institutions in the 1990s" (p. 53).

The changes since 1961 in replacement rates for the unemployed shown in figure 5.1 bear out that in all the European countries apart from Belgium and Germany the replacement rate in 1991 was substantially higher than in 1961. Such a calculation is necessarily an imperfect measure, but, being based on an average of several durations, it does take some account of the longer period of payments as well as benefit rates. Changes in generosity did not, however, all happen at the same date. The timing and the extent of the increase in replacement rates differ considerably. The OECD measure of the replacement rate in 1991 was virtually the same in Finland as in France, but in 1961 the rate in Finland was a fifth of that in France. In some countries, such as the Netherlands, the upward jump took place between 1961 and 1971; in others, such as Sweden, it took place between 1971 and 1981. Between 1981 and 1991 there were noticeable increases in Sweden, France, and Finland, but not in Denmark or Ireland.

What about the 1990s? Here the annual MISSOC reports of the European Commission are very informative. I took the reports for 1993, 1994, 1995, and 1996 (which weighed in at 7 kilograms) and traced the trends they revealed. In 1993 the commentary was in no doubt that "social protection is in crisis!", with one of the three major causes "the employment crisis" (European Commission 1994, p. 11). It goes on to note that "several countries report tighter controls over benefits to people of working age, particularly Portugal, Belgium and the Netherlands" (p. 14). These included in Belgium limiting interruption of unemployment for social or personal reasons, reinforcing penalties in event of voluntary unemployment, and restricting the system of part-time unemployment. The administration of the requirement to search for work was tightened, with the result that 35,000 people lost their entitlement to unemployment insurance in 1993 (OECD 1996, p. 43). This was followed in 1993–94 with a tightening of the contribution period and of the conditions under which young workers can claim benefit. In the Netherlands, 1993–94 saw the introduction of more stringent rules regarding the qualifying period, suitable employment and voluntary unemployment, and of a flat-rate benefit in place of earnings-related benefit where the qualifying period not fully completed.

At that time the European commentators were of the view that adjustments to unemployment benefit on the Continent would take the form of reduced coverage or tighter administration, whereas direct benefit cuts were politically difficult. However, the following year they had to eat their words: "In MISSOC 1993 it was remarked that it is difficult to cut benefits directly.... This year Germany proved that a direct approach is politically feasible" (European Commission 1995, p. 14). In Germany in 1994 the replacement rates were cut by 3 percent (1 percent for those with children), although such a reduction still appears modest by the standards of the benefit cuts in the United Kingdom, where the earnings-related supplement was completely abolished.

In 1996 the Commission returned to the pressures on unemployment benefit, noting that "[t]his benefit attracts most adverse attention during hard times.... Member states can therefore justify cutting unemployment benefits" (European Commission 1997, p. 16). They reported that the coverage or duration of benefit had been restricted in Austria, Denmark, Finland, and the Netherlands. Not all modifications were in the same direction. Belgium is reported as having slightly relaxed its conditions, allowing recipients to interrupt their availability for work for specified family or social reasons. In 1995 Finland extended unemployment benefits to cover the self-employed.

But the majority of the changes were in the direction of restricting coverage and benefits. In Austria in 1995 the Structural Adjustment Act made savings in the unemployment insurance program through a new assessment of the income of the unemployed, a reduction of family supplements extending qualifying periods, and a lowering of the replacement rate for those earning higher incomes (European Commision 1996,

p. 35). In Finland the reform package estimated to save around a quarter-billion ECUs in 1997–99 included extending the period of employment required to qualify and the freezing of benefits from 1997 to 1999.

What Has to Be Explained?

There has been considerable diversity of response to high unemployment. The United Kingdom has seriously curtailed its transfers to the unemployed, reducing both benefit levels and program coverage. In contrast, some European Union countries have made little change. In between are countries such as Austria, Belgium, Finland, Germany, and the Netherlands making significant reforms, which have largely—although not universally—served to reduce benefits and coverage.

This leads one to ask why adverse economic shocks have led countries to reduce rather than increase the provision made for those affected by unemployment. Why is it that some countries have responded more than others? There are undoubtedly a variety of motives that lie behind the provision of income maintenance to the unemployed. We need to consider the preferences of the electorate and the mechanisms by which their concerns and interests are translated into action. They may be influenced by the ideology of politicians and by the attempt of these actors to obtain and retain political power. The civil servants administering public policy may themselves have objectives they are anxious to pursue. In the field of social security, there are active pressure groups seeking to win support for their causes.

I begin by considering in section 5.2 two different interpretations of the median voter explanation of political decisions about unemployment benefit. The first is based on voters' solidarity with the unemployed; the second on prudential motives.

5.2 Voters' Support for Unemployment Benefit

Electoral politics are clearly much more complex than their representation in median voter models, where the politically chosen outcome under majority voting is that preferred by the median voter. Few issues are in fact decided by direct democracy. Moreover, the median voter theorem is not one that readily generalizes to more than one dimension. With two or more dimensions the existence of a majority voting equilibrium is problematic: in two dimensions, without tight limitations on preferences, it is possible to imagine almost any sequence of platforms, each of which obtains a majority over the previous one. The median voter model should therefore be taken more as a metaphor representing the aggregation of voter's preferences than as a direct explanation of political decisions.

Suppose that in the model of the labor market described in chapter 4 the median voter is a representative worker in the primary sector. This assumption is made for ease of exposition, but the location of the median voter is in itself an interesting question. The median voter can shift with changing employment in the two sectors or, more generally, with changes in the distribution of wages.

The employed are assumed to have some degree of concern for the level of welfare of the unemployed, and policy towards unemployment benefit reflects their wishes. The motive of the median voter may be that of solidarity with the unemployed. People in employment are, on this hypothesis, willing to pay a contribution towards unemployment benefit, reducing their own income in order to raise the income of the unemployed.

Put another way, we are supposing that people make choices according to different sets of preferences. In modeling the labor market, a person may be assumed to decide about job choices purely on the basis of personal gain, but when it comes to voting between different transfer policies, a person's own welfare depends on the welfare of others. Or it may be that people weigh considerations other than their own personal interests. Sen (1977) refers to the former as "sympathy" and the latter as "commitment." Sympathy may be seen as an instance of a consumption externality, but commitment carries with it the implication that the voter may be worse off in supporting transfers to the unemployed.

In adopting this approach, voters may be influenced by principles of social justice, including consideration of hypothetical situations such as that used to motivate either a utilitarian (Harsanyi) or maxi-min (Rawls) view of social welfare, where voters decide without knowing their personal position, only that they had an equal chance of obtaining any position in society: they decide behind what Rawls (1971) called "the veil of ignorance." In effect, voters are saying that for certain decisions one consideration that weighs with them is how they would view the world if they did not know their own position in its hierarchy.

In the present context, suppose that we represent the solidaristic preferences of the representative worker in the primary sector as

$$u\{w_p(1-t)\} + \alpha u\{b\}. \tag{5.1}$$

The welfare of a person with income x is $u\{x\}$, where $u' \geq 0$ and $u'' \leq 0$, and α measures the degree of altruism. Let us assume also that the person supposes there is an opportunity set such as that shown in figure 5.2, giving the trade-off between $(1-t)$ and the benefit level.

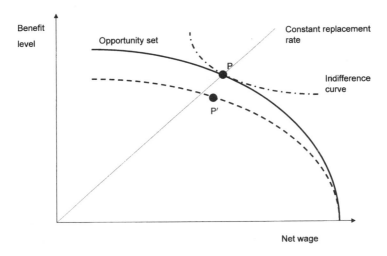

Figure 5.2
Choice made by representative worker with solidaristic preferences

The choice made by a representative worker is shown by the point P in figure 5.2, where the indifference curve is tangent to the opportunity set. For any given wage rate, this generates the net replacement rate shown by the ray through the origin. We may now ask what happens if a labor market shock leads the opportunity set to shrink: for example, where there is a rise in the number of beneficiaries. This causes the opportunity set to rotate leftwards to the dashed curve. As shown in figure 5.2 by the move from P to P', this may well lead to a fall in the desired replacement rate. As shown, benefits are cut, but there is also a tax rise so that the net wage falls, although it is of course possible that the point P' lies to the right of P so that the tax rate falls.

A sharing of the burden of higher unemployment between benefit cuts and tax rises is more likely if the increased unemployment causes the voter to attach greater weight to unemployment benefit. Suppose, for example, that concern for the unemployed is proportional to their relative numbers in the population. Then the slope of the indifference curve becomes steeper. In Atkinson 1990 I assume that the costs of transfers are proportionate, h, and show that with an iso-elastic function $u\{\ \}$ the net replacement chosen does not depend on the unemployment rate but only on α and h. A rise in the unemployment rate leads to an equiproportionate reduction in benefits and net earnings. In terms of figure 5.2, we move inwards along a ray though the origin.

In addition to the level of benefit, we need to consider the coverage of unemployment compensation. As has been argued by Davidson and Woodbury (1997) in a search model, there may be a distributional case for maximum coverage, even at the expense of reducing benefit levels, since this would transfer resources to the least advantaged. In the unemployment insurance scheme outlined in chapter 4, coverage depends on the rate at which benefit is terminated and on the extent to which secondary sector workers are covered. Given the concavity of u, there is a wide range of situations in which the preferred policy is that of maximal coverage. (The threat of disqualification for industrial misconduct remains in force, as do the initial contribution conditions.) This means that if external conditions worsen and contribution rates are unaltered, then the full effect is on the level of benefits and coverage remains unchanged. It is not easy to reconcile this with the observed reforms in Europe, where changes in coverage have predominated.

In its commentary on responses to higher unemployment, the European Commission document notes, "The unemployed attract less public sympathy than the elderly or the disabled" (European Commission 1997, p. 16). However, this on its own may not explain the benefit cuts if it was true before the rise in unemployment. What may be more relevant is a shift in voter preferences leading to a decline in the weight α attached to the welfare of the unemployed. Such a shift could have taken place as a result of political ideology. We cannot reject the hypothesis that the United Kingdom experience is best explained by a dummy variable for Mrs. Thatcher, recognizing the way in which she influenced electoral opinion, although this does not seem an entirely satisfying explanation.

On a "commitment" interpretation, it may be that the shift in preferences has involved the voter giving less weight to elements other than his or her own welfare. Priorities may have changed. Immediately after the Second World War, memories of the 1930s meant that solidaristic considerations were given considerable weight; but these tended to fade. This provides a demographic explanation. As the electorate ceased to be predominantly people who had lived through the Depression and the Second World War, so support for the welfare state waned. (The role of learning from experience is taken up below when I consider the model of redistributive politics introduced by Piketty 1995.) Inertia, too, may play a role. So long as the desirability of the postwar welfare state was not questioned, voters accepted that they should sacrifice some of their own well-being to help others, but that it was acceptance rather than positive backing. They did not oppose transfers, but if asked explicitly for an endorsement of unemployment benefits, they were not willing to provide such support. Certainly they did not feel sufficiently strongly to oppose a government that wanted on ideological grounds to roll back the welfare state.

Prudential Motives

An alternative version of the median voter model is that where concern for the unemployed stems from a prudential, insurance motive, where the employed recognize that they themselves may be future recipients. Goodin and Dryzek (1987) have argued that in fact the postwar welfare state owed a great deal to genuine risk: "[T]he pervasive uncertainty of wartime led to new popular demand for risk-spreading and [this] provides a powerful (if only a partial) explanation for the dramatic postwar upsurge in welfare states" (p. 46). (Here I am making no distinction between uncertainty and risk, although I believe it is important, not least in explaining why insurance needs to be provided publicly (on private unemployment insurance, see Barr 1988.)

In terms of the model of chapter 4, the employed place a value not just on current wages but also on the expected future receipt of benefit if their job comes to an end. From equation (4.12a), for example, we can see that for given wage rates the value of a primary sector job is a positive linear function of $(1 - t)$ and b. Adopting the assumption of chapter 4 that workers are risk neutral, so that the indifference curves shown in figure 5.3 are straight lines, we can see that this leads to a point being chosen such as P.

Even leaving aside the assumption of risk neutrality, this approach is different from that in the previous section. In the solidaristic case the uncertainty is hypothetical: the voters know full well that they are currently employed. In the prudential case the uncertainty is genuine. The idea that voters determine their policy choices behind a genuine "veil of ignorance" rather than a Rawlsian hypothetical veil affects the response to employment shocks. It may provide an explanation as to why political support for unemployment compensation declined with the onset of recession (Atkinson 1990). During the years of full employment of the 1950s and 1960s, support for the welfare state persisted, since when unemployment was low, people remained uncertain whether they would be affected if we returned to unemployment of the level of the 1930s. The unemployment rates of the 1950s and 1960s were not sufficient to provide information about the likely incidence of a major recession. By the time the rise in unemployment in the 1980s had leveled off, however, people had a much better idea as to whether or not they were likely to be at risk and what was the probability of finding another job. The veil had been lifted. The majority found that they were not at risk, and they ceased to give as much weight to the risk of unemployment in their objective function. There was a shift in the parameters of their voting preferences. In terms of equation (4.12a), there was a fall in the perceived δ_p, and a rise in the perceived μ_p, which causes the coefficient of $w_p(1-t)$ to rise relative to that of b. The preference lines in figure 5.3 become steeper, as shown, and the resulting choice could well be a lower tax rate and lower spending on unemployment benefit. It may be noted that this generates "hysteresis," in that the effect would not be reversed if unemployment were to fall.[16]

This "lifting of the veil" story may explain the reaction to a labor market shock that reduced the demand for unskilled labor and hence increased the cost of transfers. But it raises questions about the response to a second kind of shock: that which has affected the security of "good jobs," so that δ_p has in fact risen. There is a widespread perception that job insecurity has increased, but the extent to which this has actually happened is a controversial subject. In Britain its existence has been much publicized by journalists and the media; it was equally strongly denied by Conservative government ministers. In the United States some authors have identified an increase in job turnover and an associated increase in earnings instability: "There is a widespread belief that the amount of job shifting not only increased during the 1980s but that the effects of such shifting became more uncertain" (Gottschalk

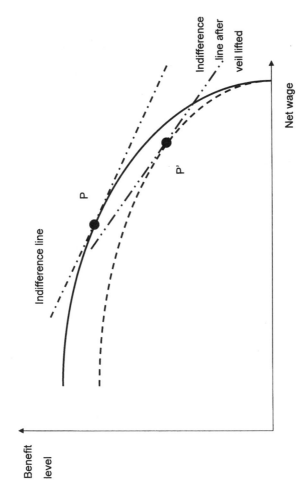

Figure 5.3
Choice made with prudential preferences

and Moffitt 1994, p. 236). Their conclusions are based on the Michigan Panel Study of Income Dynamics, but they recognize that other sources such as the Current Population Survey do not show an increase in job changing. Dickens (1994) refers to a variety of studies in the United States that do not find an increase. Munnell (1996), citing similar evidence, goes on to speculate that "if anxiety does not stem from a greater chance of being laid off, it could arise as a result of ... the changing nature of the people experiencing job loss, namely, older, white-collar, and more-educated workers who were not previously at risk" (p. 8).

It is the perceptions of job insecurity, rather than the reality, that are relevant to the political economy analysis. In stylized terms, history may have been such that first the opportunity set became less favorable on grounds of a reduced demand for unskilled workers, and that voters then reacted by adjusting their expectations and accepting benefit cuts. But this may be followed by a second stage where voters come to recognize that δ has now increased, engendering a swing back of electoral opinion as the consequences of frequent corporate re-engineering become apparent. New insecurity among primary sector workers could regenerate support for the welfare state.

Dynamics of Support for the Welfare State

The dynamics of support for the welfare state may indeed be crucial. Nearly two decades ago in his essay Some *Contradictions of the Modern Welfare State* (1984), Offe described the conservative analysis that it is "the operation of a welfare state that undermines and eventually destroys the production system upon which it has to rely in order to make its own promises come true" (p. 150). More recently, Lindbeck has emphasized that "there is a risk that the welfare state will destroy its own economic foundations. That risk is today a reality in several countries" (1995a, p. 9).

He stresses the dynamics of individual behavioral response to social transfers, arguing that disincentive effects are likely to be larger in the long run than in the short run, not least because behavior is restricted by social norms that evolve slowly over time (see also Söderström 1997). He refers to lagged adjustments in the political process, and it is with these that I am concerned here.

Suppose that the introduction of a social transfer program adjusts the tax rate, t, toward that chosen by the median voter, so that the time derivative of t is governed by

$$\dot{t} = a[t_m(\psi) - t]. \tag{5.2}$$

The tax rate, t_m, chosen by the median voter is assumed to be influenced by a degree of confidence variable, ψ, which represents the confidence that the level of benefit will be delivered. I suppose that ψ lies between 0 and 1 (inclusive), as shown in figure 5.4, with $\psi = 1$ being the case of full confidence. Where there is full confidence, the median voter's preference is the point shown by E_1 on the right-hand vertical axis in figure 5.4. The preferred tax rate falls with the degree of confidence as we move to the left, until at E_3 it falls to zero. With a prudential motive the reason for this falling support is evident: people support the program because they may be future recipients. But loss of confidence may be equally damaging where the motives are solidaristic if the concern of voters is with the delivery of benefit to the unemployed.

The degree of confidence is assumed to adjust over time according to the differential equation:

$$\dot{\psi} = \psi f(\psi, t), \tag{5.3}$$

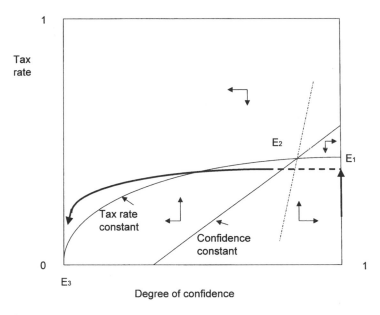

Figure 5.4
Dynamics of support for welfare state

where $f(\ )$ increases with ψ and decreases with t. In other words, the degree of confidence increases as confidence increases (i.e., it feeds on itself) but decreases as the tax rate increases. A high tax rate is considered to be evidence that the system is unsustainable, and there is a maximum tax rate consistent with full confidence being maintained, shown on the vertical axis in figure 5.4 above E_1. There are three possible equilibria:

1. E_1, with 100% confidence and the median voter's preferred tax rate (at $\psi = 1$),

2. E_2, an interior solution, which is a saddlepoint and not therefore generally attained (the arms of the saddlepoint, the

sole trajectories along which it is approached, are shown by
the dashed and dotted line),

3. E_3, with no taxation and zero benefit.

The outcome depends on the initial conditions, and by the
same token is subject to the influence of extraneous shocks. To
tell only one of the possible stories, suppose that the economy
is approaching the equilibrium E_1 in figure 5.4, with full confidence and the tax rate rising to its long-run value, as indicated
by the heavy line. Alarms are then raised, by economists perhaps, about the hazards of the welfare state. This causes a
large instantaneous drop in public confidence, taking us leftwards in figure 5.4, as indicated by the dashed line. As shown,
this takes us beyond the upward converging arm of the saddlepoint, E_2. As a result the economy then diverges towards
the zero tax, zero welfare state equilibrium.

   This story should not be taken too seriously, but I feel that
there is something to be said for it, not least that it allows
economists, normally shy of surfacing in their own theories, to
make an appearance in the model of the political process. And
there are other, more subtle theories, such as that advanced by
Piketty (1995).[17] He models redistribution by majority voting
in a world of successive dynasties where voters hold beliefs
about the role of inequality and opportunity and of effort in
determining pre-tax incomes. People differ in their beliefs and
update these beliefs in the light of their own income. Heterogeneity of beliefs persists in the long run. As Piketty (1995)
notes, "The multiplicity of steady states explains ... why different countries can remain in different redistributive equilibria, although the underlying structural parameters of mobility
are essentially the same" (p. 554).

   He points to the question—particularly interesting in the
present context—of the implications in this model of changes

in the economic fundamentals. What are the effects of one generation being subjected to an unemployment shock?

5.3   Alternatives to Voting Explanations

The explanations considered to date treat as decisive the preferences of the median voter. The extent to which the preferences of voters are translated into policy is, however, limited by a degree of "slack" in the political process. In practice there is freedom of manoeuvre for politicians and civil servants, who interpret the mandate they have been given by the electorate. The shift in social transfer policy may be due to the reactions of politicians and civil servants rather than any shift in the preferences of the electorate. It may be due to the operations of pressure or lobby groups.

Policy is not after all made in binding referenda; rather, it is made by politicians elected on broad platforms for terms of office of several years. If one reads accounts of election campaigns, and campaign documents, then there have indeed been occasions when social security issues have featured prominently. McGovern made promises regarding a negative income tax. United States presidential candidates have often talked of reforming welfare. In the United Kingdom there have been explicit promises with regard to the level of pensions, as when Labour won the 1974 election, or child benefit, as when Labour lost the 1992 election. The Rocard government was elected on a pledge to introduce a guaranteed minimum income. The Portuguese government elected in 1995 made a similar proposal. But there are many occasions when other issues have dominated the election campaign. Moreover, policy has to be made for three, four, five, or even seven years, between elections. Governments have to respond to events.

The shocks to which they are reacting may not have been apparent when the election took place.

Agencies

Policy is put into effect by civil servants and may be administered by semi-independent or even independent agencies. In the case of social security, there are a wide variety of arrangements, as is illustrated in table 5.1, which covers unemployment insurance and pension administration. The bodies responsible for the carrying out of transfer payments include central government departments, local offices of central bodies, local authorities, insurance institutes, trade unions, and agencies. These bodies may be directly answerable to the ministry or they may be self-governing, with representation from the social partners.

Political slack appears particularly likely in areas of complexity like social security. As is pointed out by Musgrave and Musgrave, "public programs are complex and elected officials may have neither the time nor the expertise to analyze them. That branch of the government which is backed by technical experts is thus at a great advantage" (1989, p. 103). This consideration may apply more to certain levels of policy than to others. The public visibility of benefit *levels*, for example, may mean that these are decided ultimately by politicians, whereas more detailed decisions affecting the *coverage* of benefit may be more influenced by civil servants. Here ministers may not be able to assess the degree of preselection that has taken place in the menu of choices with which they are offered.

There is a parallel with the corporation, where the owners of the firm are unable to exercise full control over the management, which allows the latter some scope to pursue their own objectives. The owners do not have the technical knowledge or the knowledge of what is happening on the spot necessary to maintain full control. There is an asymmetry of information which gives rise to a principal-agent problem. The design of appropriate incentive schemes has given rise to a large literature (for reviews of the literature in general, see, for example, Laffont and Tirole 1993 and Armstrong, Cowan, and Vickers 1994). Where the agent is risk-averse, the optimal incentive scheme typically offers some insurance to the agent and less than 100 percent of marginal profits, reducing the power of the incentive scheme to induce the agent to follow the wishes of the principal. The results depend on the formulation, but the position for a simple class of models is summarized by Tirole (1989) as follows:

[E]ffort, if not observed, must be induced through incentives. The manager's wage must grow with the realized profit. Because such incentive structures destroy insurance, the expected wage bill required to obtain effort is higher under nonobservability. This, in turn, may make the shareholders not wish to induce effort; that is, they may tolerate slacking" (p. 38).

As, however, Dixit has pointed out in the first Munich Lectures in Economics, "agency relationships are often more complex in the political than in the economic context" (1996, p. 52). He notes that it is not clear who is the agent and who is the principal. It could be that the voters are the principals and the elected politicians the agents, or the politicians the principals and civil servants the agents, or the civil servants the principals and independent agencies (such as an independent central bank, or the Benefits Agency in the United Kingdom, or UNEDIC in France) the agents. Drawing on the work of Wilson (1989), Dixit argues that each agency typically deals with several principals. A social security agency, for example, is answerable to the government, but may also have regard

Table 5.1a
Administration of unemployment benefits

Country	Ministry	Administration	Representation
Belgium	Ministry of Employment and Labor	National Employment Office; payments by trade union organization or Auxiliary Fund	Employees and employers
Denmark	Ministry of Labor	Unemployment insurance funds	
Germany	Federal Ministry of Labor and Social Affairs	Federal Institute for Employment	Employees, employers, and public governments
Greece	Ministry of Labor and Social Security	Office for Employment and Manpower	Insured, pensioners, employers, and State
Spain	Ministry of Labor and Social Security	National Employment Office	Supervised by National and Regional Councils (representatives of employees, employers, and public administration)
France	Ministry of Labor, Social Dialogue, and Participation	UNEDIC/ASSEDIC	Employees and employers
Ireland	Department of Social Welfare	Social Welfare Services Office	
Italy	Ministry of Labor and Social Welfare	National Social Welfare Institute	

			Employees and employers
Luxembourg	Ministry of Labor	Labor Administration	
Netherlands	Ministry of Social Affairs	Industrial Boards	
Austria	Federal Ministry of Labor and Social Affairs	Labor market Services	
Portugal	Ministry of Labor and Social Security	Regional employment offices	
Finland	Ministry of Social Affairs and Health, *and* Ministry of Labor	Unemployment insurance funds, and Social Insurance Institution	
Sweden	Ministry of Labor	Unemployment insurance funds	
United Kingdom	Department of Social Security	Employment Service	

Source: European Commission 1996.

Table 5.1b
Administration of retirement or old age pensions

Country	Ministry	Administration	Representation
Belgium	Ministry of Social Security	National Pension Office	Employees and employers
Denmark	Ministry of Social Affairs	Local authorities	
Germany	Federal Ministry of Labor and Social Affairs	Range of self-governing Federal and Länder institutions	Employees and employers
Greece	Ministry of Labor and Social Security	Institute for Social Insurance	Insured, pensioners, employers and State
Spain	Ministry of Labor and Social Security	National Social Security Office	Supervised by National and Regional Councils (representatives of employees, employers and public administration)
France	Ministry of Public Health and Health Insurance, *and* Ministry of Solidarity between the Generations	National Old Age Insurance funds	
Ireland	Department of Social Welfare	Social Welfare Services Office	
Italy	Ministry of Labor and Social Welfare	National Social Welfare Institute	

Luxembourg	Ministry of Social Security	4 pension institutions	Social partners
Netherlands	Ministry of Social Affairs	Social Insurance Bank	Employees and employers
Austria	Federal Ministry of Labor and Social Affairs	7 pension insurance funds (self-governing)	
Portugal	Ministry of Labor and Social Security	National Pensions Fund	
Finland	Ministry of Social Affairs and Health	Central Pension Security Institute	
Sweden	Ministry of Health and Social Affairs	National Social Insurance Board	
United Kingdom	Department of Social Security	Benefits Agency	

Source: European Commission 1996.

to individual members of Parliament, to representatives of claimant groups, to trade unions, and to public opinion. This multiplicity of principals is institutionalized where there are representatives of the social partners (see the final column of table 5.1). Dixit goes on to argue that where there are several principals, the power of incentive schemes is weakened. It can also be conjectured that the existence of multiple principals may reduce the degree of response to changes in external circumstances. The need for agreement on changes in benefit regulations may put sand in the machinery, and hence explain why certain countries have responded less to increased levels of unemployment.

Where there is slack in the system, how do the agents choose to make use of it? It is presumably not simply a matter of minimizing effort; civil servants, for instance, may have their own rewards from the agency's activities and their own objectives. Can we explain in this way a shift in social security policy? One explanation that cannot account for the observed shift to a smaller welfare state is the popularly made assumption that civil servants aim for growth. Just as corporate managers are assumed to like to see their branches grow, since it gives them prestige and power, so too it has been argued that reputation, power, and patronage for civil servants derives in an analogous way from the size of their budget. Therefore, civil servants attempt to promote the activities of their department; they compete with other civil servants for funds and influence, seeking to take over new functions and to retain existing powers. (Since expansion involves effort and decision making, this is likely to run in the opposite direction from that assumed in the contract literature, where the effort-minimizing activity will typically be to preserve the status quo.) This idea has been developed by Brennan and Buchanan (1977, 1978), who have argued that the state machinery as a whole will seek to act like a Leviathan, aiming to maximize the size of the government department or agency.

The theory described above makes strong assumptions about the motives of government officials. It is not in fact obvious that the motives of the civil servant will all be towards expansion. It may be that personal success is judged in a different way. Civil servants anxious to further their careers may do better by reducing the expenditure; they may recognize that a growing budget renders them exposed in budgetary negotiations. Faced with increased unemployment, they might respond by seeking to remain within a specified budget and seek to identify ways to reduce recipient numbers. Moreover, the self-interest view of government bureaucracy seems an oversimplified one. As Musgrave has written, "maximisation may involve targets other than personal economic gain and power (e.g. duty, respect of one's colleagues, realisation of what one considers to be a 'good society', and the satisfaction of having contributed thereto" (1986, p. 209). They may, for example, be persuaded by seminars given by prominent economists that social transfers have adverse economic consequences, and seek to reduce their coverage in order to limit what they perceive to be economic damage.

The political slack explanation may also be relevant if there have been changes in the extent of such slack. In the United Kingdom, where changes in benefit policy have been extensive, there have also been major shifts in organizational structure. The move to a more delegated agency pattern of management may have tightened the control of politicians, able now to set explicit managerial objectives to agency heads, rather than allowing civil servants to pursue a broader notion of the public interest. A comparative analysis would in this respect be especially rewarding, since different countries have made different changes, or no change at all, in their administrative structures.

Pressure Groups

Social security programs have often been taken as exemplars of a policy area where special interest groups can bring to bear both political muscle and command of policy detail. They have been present right from the early days. Skocpol describes how in the United States, "After the Civil War, hundreds of thousands of former Union soldiers organized themselves into veterans' associations, which in turn repeatedly lobbied Congress to improve benefits" (1995, p. 50). She expresses doubts as to the extent of the impact and argues that the Arrears Act may have stimulated the associations as much as vice versa; but with a membership, at its peak, of 39% of all surviving Union veterans, the Grand Army of the Republic was potentially an important political force. Pressure groups were often in conflict, as illustrated in the United Kingdom at the turn of the nineteenth century by the National Committee of Organised Labour for Promoting Old Age Pensions, opposed by the Charity Organisation Society, which advocated the traditional approach (Heclo 1974, p. 168).

The role of pressure or interest groups has long been analyzed in the political science literature, and influential contributions by economists include Olson (1965) and Becker (1983). Becker has applied his model of competition among pressure groups to the expansion of public spending. Asking how the rapid increase in transfer payments could be explained, he says that "an important part of the answer is found in changes in the access to political influence of the old, ill, and other beneficiaries of transfer payments" (1985, p. 345).

In the present context, we need to turn the explanation round and ask why it is that in some cases pressure groups have been successful in protecting expenditure against governments seeking to cut transfers, whereas other beneficiaries have not been shielded in this way. Suppose we apply a version of the Becker model to the situation of a transfer of b to each of the U unemployed financed equally by L workers. Following Becker (1985), the scale of the program is

$$bU = I[p_u, p_w, U/L], \qquad (5.4)$$

where I is the influence function, p_u is the political pressure exercised by the unemployed, and p_w is the pressure of the workers. Influence is an increasing function of pressure, and pressure is exerted by expenditure on political activities. Political leverage is assumed to be a positive function of numbers in the sense that I is an increasing function of U/L, but Becker cautions that this does not imply that an increase in the number of beneficiaries will raise the size of the transfer, since the political pressure p_i is negatively related to numbers. Becker attributes this to free-riding behavior or greater costs of organization. A rise in unemployment could therefore, depending on the precise assumptions, lead to reduced political pressure by the unemployed (and increased mobilization by the employed), so that the total program is reduced.[18]

One cannot, however, help feeling that the crucial elements are those that are contained within the "black box" of the influence function. The political role of the unemployed is not just a matter of the cost of financing lobbying activity. Moreover, the influence of pressure groups itself depends on decisions by the government. As Skocpol noted in the case of Union veterans, legislation enhanced the role of the associations. Regulation of transfers, whether public or private, may generate a payoff to collective action, a point to which I return when discussing private pensions. The powers of trade unions, one of the potential defenders of unemployment benefit, have been modified as part of moves to a flexible labor market. They are also affected by labor market conditions, as assumed in chapter 3; the same forces that have led to mass unemployment have weakened the political support given to the unemployed.

5.4 Conclusion

The political economy of the welfare state is important in its own right and because it is linked to the analysis of the economic consequence of reform. It is for this reason that I have included this chapter, sandwiched as it is between models of the labor market and models of economic growth. The issues raised are, however, much more than can be treated in a single chapter. The phenomenon to explain is complex. European countries are not marching in step. The expansion of the welfare state took place at different dates and in different circumstances. Nor is the history of recent years a simple dichotomy between the United Kingdom, with its far-reaching cuts, and the rest of the European Union, making only marginal adjustments. Countries have differed in the scale and form of their responses to high unemployment. In seeking to explain social transfer policy, we need to have recourse to a variety of explanations. Different models have different implications and need to be set side by side. Insofar as the welfare state is being rolled back, this may reflect a shift in voter preferences, either exogenous or endogenous where there has been a "lifting of the veil" following the rise in unemployment. The dynamics of the welfare state may have been fundamentally changed by the alarms raised about the feasibility of its continuance. If there is political slack, then the explanation may be found in politicians' preferences and in the objectives of civil servants. It may be that there has been a shift in the balance, with agencies acquiring greater power and civil servants less. The power of pressure groups may have shifted against the unemployed. In developing these explanations, economists need to draw both on their microanalytic skills and on the wealth of literature in political science. The political economy of the welfare state is a fascinating challenge to social scientists to cross disciplinary boundaries.

6   Savings, Pensions, and Economic Growth

From levels of output and employment, I now move to the trend rate of growth. Would a cut in welfare state spending stimulate economic growth? In this and the next chapter, I concentrate simply on this question. I do not ask whether an increase in growth is desirable nor about the optimal rate of growth. A faster growth rate may lower social welfare according to a specified set of objectives. Here I am not investigating such "welfare" issues. In terms of the "GDP versus welfare" distinction of chapter 3, it is the former—in its dynamic version—with which I am concerned here.

In order to assess the mechanisms by which the welfare state may affect the growth of the economy, we need a suitable theoretical framework. The competitive general equilibrium model with which I started in chapter 3 may be given a dynamic interpretation, assuming a full set of futures markets, but this neither coincides with the reality of existing markets nor captures the interesting features of a dynamic economy. Here, instead, I make use of the theory of economic growth, in which there has been a resurgence of interest in the past decade.[19]

In considering the impact on growth of social transfers, I concentrate on the case of retirement pensions. I make little

Table 6.1
Pensions as percentage of total benefit expenditure, 1986

Portugal	74.2
Switzerland	64.9
Austria	58.2
United States	57.1
New Zealand	55.2
Australia	53.4
Spain	51.1
Germany (West)	50.1
Netherlands	48.7
United Kingdom	46.0
France	44.1
Norway	42.5
Denmark	42.4
Sweden	42.1
Belgium	33.5
Canada	33.1
Ireland	29.1

Source: ILO 1992, table 10.
Note: Figures for Canada are for 1985.

apology for so doing, since pensions form the largest single component of most social security budgets. In the United States, Social Security is the largest federal government spending program. According to the ILO cost of social security tables (ILO 1992), pensions form more than half of total benefit expenditure in eight of the OECD countries shown in table 6.1, and in a further six it exceeds 40 percent. (It is not of course always easy to draw clear distinctions between different types of expenditure; the figures are only an indication.) Pensions are certainly one of the most discussed aspects of social security. The Richard *T.* Ely Lecture to the American Economic Association by Martin Feldstein (1996), entitled "The Missing Piece in Policy Analysis: Social Security Reform," refers almost exclusively to pensions. At the same time, we need to bear in mind that other transfers may affect savings and investment. This applies, for example, to sickness and disability benefits, which may affect the level of precautionary savings. Pensions have also to be seen in relation to the provision of long-term care for the elderly, an issue that is likely to receive increasing attention.

6.1 Savings and Growth

In order to study the dynamics of the economy, I now simplify in other respects. I consider an aggregate economy with a single sector of production. There is assumed to be no home production, no self-employment, and there is no segmentation of the labor market. All workers are identical and all are fully employed at a market clearing wage, w. Capital is fully employed and earns a rate of return, r. For simplicity, I take the aggregate Cobb-Douglas production function used earlier:

$$Y = K^{\beta}[AL]^{(1-\beta)}, \tag{6.1}$$

where Y denotes GDP, K denotes capital, L denotes labor, and A now denotes the level of labor productivity, assumed to depend on the level of technical knowledge. It should be noted that with the Cobb-Douglas function no distinction may be drawn between technical progress that tends to make labor more productive and technical progress that makes capital more productive. (The representation in (6.1) is chosen simply for expositional purposes).

How may the welfare state affect the growth rate? The different channels may be seen if we use (6.1) to write the growth rate as

$$g_Y = \beta g_K + (1 - \beta)(g_A + n), \tag{6.2}$$

where g_X denotes the proportionate growth rate of the variable X, and the labor supply is assumed to be growing over time at a constant rate n (taken to be zero in much of what follows). The first possible mechanism is via a reduction in the savings rate and in capital accumulation. In terms of the earlier discussion (in chapter 2) of the empirical literature, this would show up as an effect on the total rate of growth, not on factor productivity: that is, g_K rather than g_A. If S denotes savings and there is assumed to be no depreciation of capital, then

$$g_K = S/K = (S/Y)/(K/Y). \tag{6.3}$$

A reduction of the savings rate (S/Y), denoted later by s, reduces the immediate growth rate. What happens subsequently depends on the evolution of the capital-output ratio, K/Y. In the (Solow) neoclassical growth model, if S/Y were to fall, then over time the capital output ratio falls, and in steady state the fall in (K/Y) fully offsets the fall in the savings ratio, leaving the growth rate unchanged. A reduction in the savings rate lowers the level of output but does not affect the steady state rate of growth. This may be seen by setting $g_Y = g_K$ in equation (6.2):

$$g_Y = g_K \quad \text{implies} \quad g_Y = g_A + n. \tag{6.4}$$

The steady state growth rate at which output and capital are growing at the same rate is equal to the rate of population growth plus the rate of technical progress. In the long run (and the speed of convergence may be slow), any decline in savings induced by the welfare state does not affect the growth rate in the Solow neoclassical growth model.

If, however, the rate of technical progress is treated as endogenous rather than exogenous, then the transfer system may affect the long-run growth rate. This possibility has been much analyzed in the post-1985 growth theory literature, although the idea of endogenous technical progress originated much earlier (see, for example, the survey article Hahn and Matthews 1964). Suppose that we take the simple version of the Arrow (1962) learning by doing model, where productivity A depends on experience, which is proportional to cumulated past investment, or K. This gives a production function for the economy as a whole such that there are constant social returns to capital:

$$Y = a^* K[L]^{(1-\beta)} \equiv a(L)K. \tag{6.5}$$

This is referred to below as the "AK" model. If the total labor force, L, is assumed constant (i.e., $a(L)$ is a constant), then the economy is in instantaneous steady growth at rate

$$g = g_Y = g_K = S/K = sa(L). \tag{6.6}$$

A rise in the savings rate, s, leads to a permanently increased rate of growth and a corresponding increase in the rate of technical progress. On this steady growth path, the competitive share of capital is β, and the output-capital ratio is a, so that the private competitive return to capital, r, is equal to $a\beta$. This is constant if L is constant (Romer 1996, p. 119). The wage rate is equal to

$$w = (1 - \beta)Y/L = (1 - \beta)a(L)/L \cdot K, \tag{6.7}$$

so that if L is constant the wage rate grows at rate g.

The two models just described do not do justice to the richness of growth theory, but they illustrate clearly the distinction between the two hypotheses identified in chapter 2 (and illustrated in figure 2.4). According to the Solow model, a rise in the savings rate raises the long-run level of GDP but not the trend growth rate, whereas according to the ΛK model, the rise in the savings rate leads to a permanently increased rate of growth. In the short run they may be indistinguishable, but in the long run they are very different. It is the long run that appears to have particular hold on the public imagination, and I concentrate here on the AK model, despite its evident limitations (the unsatisfactory features of this formulation are clearly brought out by Solow 1994).

6.2   State Pensions and Growth

What can we conclude from this about the impact of social transfers? To consider this, we need to investigate the determinants of saving behavior. Much of modern growth theory assumes that this can be modeled in terms of a representative agent maximizing the integral of discounted utility over an infinite horizon. This "Ramsey" formulation requires that the rate of growth of consumption, and hence the steady state growth rate of capital, equals

$$g = (r_n - \rho)/\varepsilon, \tag{6.8}$$

where r_n is the return to individuals net of any taxes, ρ is the rate of discount, and $1/\varepsilon$ the rate of intertemporal substitution in the utility function. If we follow the herd in making this assumption, then the impact of social transfers can only operate via the net rate of return (bearing in mind that the gross rate of return is fixed at $a\beta$ in the AK model). The payment of a state pension financed by a payroll tax that does not affect r_n has no impact on the desired growth rate of capital. As pointed out by Bertola (1993), we have a situation resembling the extreme Kaldorian model (Kaldor 1956), where savings are proportionate to capital income, and the rate of growth of capital is equal to the savings rate times the rate of return. None of the income accruing to nonaccumulated factors is saved.

Neither the Ramsey nor the extreme Kaldorian models seem particularly appealing as explanations of savings in modern economies. More commonly used in studies of the impact of pensions have been models of life-cycle savings with a finite lifetime and no bequests (so that there is no Ricardian equivalence). One such is the discrete time overlapping generations model of Samuelson (1958), as elaborated by Diamond (1965), where people, identical in all respects apart from their date of birth, live for two periods working for a wage w during the first and living off their savings in the second. The capital available to the next generation is equal to the savings of the preceding generation of workers. This model is used, for example, in Diamond 1997 to examine the implications of building up a trust fund for social security.[20] In such real-world policy applications, one needs to take account of the demographic structure, but here I simply assume a constant population.

To make the overlapping generations model more precise, let us suppose that people choose to consume in the first period of their lives a fraction $(1 - \sigma)$ of their net present discounted receipts, which are equal to the wage net of payroll tax at rate t plus the pension, b, received next period discounted by $(1 + r)$, since the net return is equal to the gross return. This may be seen as the result of maximizing the Cobb-Douglas utility function

$$U(c_1, c_2) = c_1^{(1-\sigma)} c_2^{\sigma},\qquad(6.9)$$

(where $0 < \sigma < 1$) subject to the budget constraint

$$c_1 + c_2/(1 + r) = w - tw + b/(1 + r).\qquad(6.10)$$

State pay-as-you-go pensions may be seen as a contract between two overlapping generations. Transfers are paid from
the contributions of the working generation to those who
have retired, with the amount received by each person proportional to his or her individual contribution. Pensions are
discounted by a factor $(1 + r)$; on the other hand, they are
expected to be higher than when the contributors were young
on account of rising average incomes (and growing population, although this is assumed away here). If the pension
scheme is assumed to be in steady state with a constant tax
rate, the pension received per head is the contribution (tw)
increased by a factor $(1 + g)$, since in the next period the wage
bill is higher by this amount (g is the growth rate of the wage
bill). This means that the right hand side of the individual
budget constraint may be written:

$$w - tw + tw(1+g)/(1+r) = w - tw(r-g)/(1+r). \quad (6.11)$$

The pay-as-you-go scheme makes people worse or better off
according to whether the rate of interest obtainable on private
savings is greater or less than the rate of growth. Where the
rate of growth is equal to the rate of discount $(g = r)$, these
two effects cancel, as in the celebrated result of Samuelson
(1958, 1975) and Aaron (1966). If the rate of growth is equal
to the rate of discount, then, given our assumptions, a worker
values the package with social insurance taxes and benefits the
same as that without. However, this does not mean that savings are unaffected. The capital carried forward by individuals
is

$$sw \equiv w(1 - t) - (1 - \sigma)w[1 - t(r - g)/(1 + r)]$$

$$= [\sigma - t + (1 - \sigma)t(r - g)/(1 + r)]w. \quad (6.12)$$

We can see that where $r = g$ the payroll tax would have a pure pay-as-you-go effect, with state contributions displacing private savings at the rate of one euro for one euro.

The situation where the growth rate is less than the rate of return is illustrated in figure 6.1. From (6.11) we can see that the budget line with the state pension lies inside that with no state pension. The points chosen by a person with a constant savings propensity are shown by P, in the absence of the state pension scheme, and P' with the pension and tax. As may be seen from the diagram, the reduction in private savings is less than tw, since the level of consumption in period 1 is reduced (the person being worse off, since the state pension offers a lower return ($g < r$)). On the other hand, the reduction in savings is greater than σtw, as may be seen from writing

$$s = \sigma(1 - t) - t(1 - \sigma)(1 + g)/(1 + r). \tag{6.13}$$

This means that the pension scheme has a greater negative effect on savings than would a simple tax at rate t; it is not therefore purely the fiscal impact that is in operation but a specific feature of the pension provision: it displaces part of private savings.

Combined with the AK learning by doing model used above, assuming a constant labor force L, this savings rate determines the rate of growth. The capital stock in the next period is $(1 + g)K$, and this equals the savings of the current working generation (the retired generation are dissaving). The savings are given by swL, which in turn equal $s(1 - \beta)aK$. Hence:

$$(1 + g) = s(1 - \beta)a(L). \tag{6.14}$$

(It may be noted that g appears on the right hand side of (6.14) via s.) If we were to start from a position where the rate of growth equals the rate of return, then we have seen that the

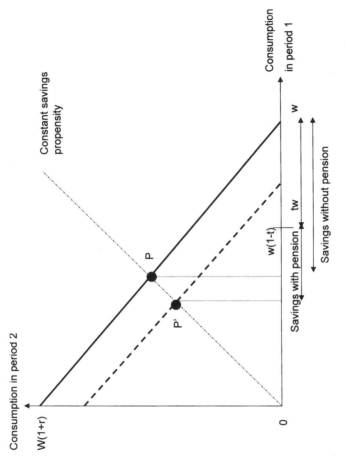

Figure 6.1
Impact of pay-as-you-go state pension on private savings

payroll tax would simply displace private savings and hence reduce the rate of growth. Where the initial rate of growth is less than the rate of return the effect is smaller, but the savings rate is still reduced.

The above analysis applies to a scheme in steady state. Where the scheme is building up, then the present value of benefits may exceed the value of contributions, as where older workers are "blanketed in"—given pension entitlements, for example, in excess of the actuarial value of their contributions. In a pay-as-you-go scheme, where current contributions finance current benefits, the rate of "return" equals the growth of the tax base (typically the wage bill), and where the scheme is being extended to new groups this can exceed the rate of growth of the economy as a whole. Where the scheme has reached maturity the "rate of return" falls, and this is one reason why financing problems have become apparent.

The concerns expressed about the financing problems of social security have in turn led to doubts as to whether the present level of benefits can be maintained. Recently a firm of actuaries in the United Kingdom published a ranking of the "level of security" attached to different forms of pension provision. (The details of the methods were not given.) It is not perhaps surprising that a personal pension, based on private financial institution, with no guaranteed benefits, had a level of security of 65 percent. What is surprising is that the state pension had a ranking of only 85 percent (the same as for an employer's final salary scheme). Doubts are now present in people's minds that would have been inconceivable twenty-five years ago. This links back to the political economy model of the previous chapter.

In the models just described, labor supply in the first period is assumed to be fixed. The model may be extended to allow for variation in the date of retirement. As has been shown by

Feldstein (1976a), if a reduction in the state pension causes people to stay at work longer, this then reduces the need for life-cycle savings. It is for this reason that he concludes that in theory "the net effect of social security on the saving of the non-aged is indeterminate" (p. 78).

Leaving aside this qualification concerning retirement age, we have described a situation in which the welfare state can have an adverse impact on the long-run growth rate. The existence of a state pension scheme reduces savings, and the reduction in the savings rate can, with the AK model, reduce the long-run rate of growth (and with the neoclassical model, there is an immediate reduction in the growth rate). This does not, however, mean that the scaling back of the state pay-as-you-go scheme would necessarily raise the growth rate. It depends what was put in its place. As noted in chapter 3, we need to consider the alternatives.

6.3   Replacing State Pensions by a Means-Tested Safety Net

Those advocating cuts in state pensions do not usually propose that nothing take its place. Critics wish to see a better targeting of state spending, with the public pay-as-you-go pension being scaled back or state provision being replaced by private pensions. The thrust of the World Bank (1994) document, *Averting the Old Age Crisis*, with its "three pillar" approach, is in these directions. The public pillar would remain, but with the limited object of alleviating old-age poverty, and there would be a mandatory funded second pillar, privately managed. (The third pillar is additional voluntary savings.) These do not of course exhaust the reform possibilities. For example, in the United States reform proposals include the funding of part of the state pension via investment in the equity market, and the introduction of personal social security accounts (Diamond 1996 and Gramlich 1996). A convenient summary of different United States reform proposals is provided by Engen and Gale (1997, table 1); the same volume (Sass and Triest 1997) contains accounts of reforms in Mexico, the United Kingdom, Australia, and Japan.

Policy reforms would have economic consequences. If greater targeting means replacing universal pensions by means-tested benefits, then this affects the incentives faced by households. The growth of private pension funds has consequences for the working of the capital market. In this section I consider the implications of means testing; the replacement by private pensions is taken up in the next chapter.

Suppose that the level of state pension provided to those with no other resources is left unchanged but that the state benefit is withdrawn progressively from those with other sources of income. The pension ceases to be universal and becomes an "assistance pension." In a limiting case, the state benefit represents a minimum income guarantee and is reduced at a rate of one euro for one euro of other resources. Such a reform promises to reduce total public expenditure while still meeting the antipoverty objective (providing the guarantee is set at a sufficient level). But the test of resources changes the intertemporal budget constraint faced by the individual. People who prior to retirement foresee that increased savings lead to reduced state transfers may adjust their savings behavior. In the case of the minimum income guarantee, they in effect face an either/or choice: either they save sufficiently to be completely independent in old age or they reduce their savings to zero and rely solely on the state benefit.

Such a policy move toward assistance pensions, although reducing total welfare state spending, creates a "savings trap." The potential impact may be seen in the earlier two-period model. Figure 6.2 shows the choice now faced by the individual when there is a minimum income guarantee. (The guarantee is assumed to apply to the level of consumable resources: i.e., there is an assets test as well as an income test.) Suppose that the minimum guarantee is set at the level of the previous pay-as-you-go pension, $tw_{av}(1 + g)$: that is, a proportion t of the average wage, allowing for the fact that this rises at rate $(1 + g)$. The switch to an assistance pension allows the tax rate levied on earnings, τ, to be less than the previous value t, since the guarantee is paid to only a fraction of pensioners. As shown in figure 6.2, the opportunity set is now nonconvex, and the consumer compares the highest level of utility obtainable on the dashed line leading up from the point B with that obtainable at point D, consuming the entire net wage in the first period and the minimum pension in the second. In the case shown, the indifference curve touching AB at P cuts the BD line, so that D would be preferred. From the utility function (6.9), we can calculate that the minimum pension is preferable where

$$w < t/(1 - \tau) \cdot w_{av}h \cdot (1 + g)/(1 + r), \tag{6.15}$$

where h is a constant greater than 1.

To understand the implications of this proposal, we can no longer rely on the assumption of representative identical individuals but have to treat explicitly distributional differences. These involve first of all differences in wage rates. For people with wage rates above the critical value in (6.15), savings rise on two counts. First, the tax rate is lower. Second, the contribution is a pure tax, so that they reduce present consumption correspondingly: the savings rate is reduced not by t but by $\sigma\tau$. On the other hand, for those with wage rates below the critical value, savings are reduced to zero. Whether or not aggregate savings increase depends on the number of people

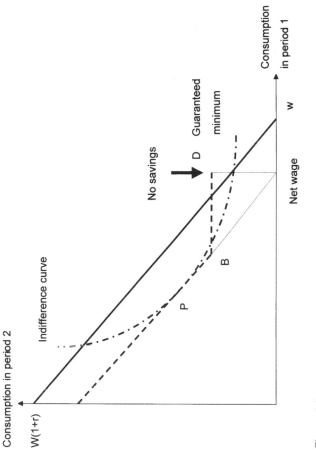

Figure 6.2
Effect of minimum income guarantee

above and below the cutoff, their relative wages, and the other parameters. The net impact is unclear.

Heterogeneity arises secondly on account of differences in attitudes towards savings. This is treated by Feldstein (1987) in his welfare analysis of the choice between means-tested and universal pensions. He assumes that the population is divided into a group of identical people who save for their old age, according to the lifecycle process as described above, and a group of otherwise identical people who make no financial provision for old age. The level of the means-tested benefit is constrained by the requirement that the former group continue to save. This means that the maximum tax rate, with a Cobb-Douglas utility function and $\sigma = \frac{1}{2}$, is given by

$$\mu/[\mu + 4(1 + g)/(1 + r)], \qquad (6.16)$$

where μ is the proportion of nonsavers. The maximum replacement rate in terms of wages for the nonsavers is

$$(1 + g)/[\mu + 4(1 + g)/(1 + r)]. \qquad (6.17)$$

So that if the growth rate equals the rate of return and equals 1 per generation, and a third of the population are nonsavers, then the maximum tax rate is $1/13$ and the maximum replacement rate $6/13$.

It does not, however, seem particularly realistic to suppose that the population is rigidly divided into savers and nonsavers (and Feldstein introduces a third group later in his article). Indeed it may be questioned whether we want to rely on exogenously introduced differences in savings behavior. The model described earlier, with a continuous distribution of wages, allows the class of nonsavers to be determined endogenously. People for whom saving is not attractive are those satisfying (6.15), the right-hand side of which is an increasing function of t and τ. We can see how concerns arise about the welfare state creating its own dependants. Such concerns do not of course arise with universal pensions. It is ironic if the welfare state should be attacked for creating dependency when pre-welfare state assistance elements are largely responsible.

The savings trap could be thought to be of little practical importance, but it is beginning to receive widespread attention. In the United Kingdom, Watsons, the actuaries, published a study of the impact of means-tested benefits on occupational pensions (Collins 1993). They contrasted the position of a person who had no occupational pension with that of a colleague who had a pension from his previous employer of £6 a week. As a result of the withdrawal of means-tested benefits, the latter was only 87p a week better off. This represents a marginal tax rate of 85.5 percent. There was in fact little net gain from the occupational pension until it reached some £50 a week.

For those with private savings the position is even more serious. A person in the United Kingdom with savings in excess of a specified amount (£8,000 in 1997) is not eligible for means-tested assistance (Income Support); and those with savings between this amount and a lower figure (£3,000) are assumed to be receiving a weekly "tariff" income equal to £1 for every £250. This corresponds to an assumed return of over 20 percent. As a result, it is actually a disadvantage to have income from saving. Figure 6.3 shows the net income of pensioners with different amounts of capital, assuming a 5 percent rate of return. There is a definite savings trap. Net income with zero savings is higher than that with savings up to that generating an income of some £50 a week, which was of the order of the basic state pension at that time. This diagram is based on the work of Hills, who comments, "If people realise that they will face this position in advance, they may decide there is little point in saving or building up pension rights be-

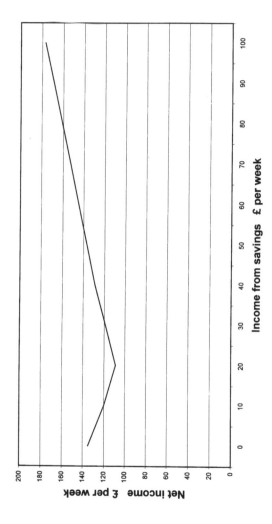

Figure 6.3
Savings trap for pensioners in the United Kingdom. Source: Hills 1993, figure 20. The figures relate to 1993–94 and to a pensioner couple who are tenants.

low a threshold" (1993, p. 29). In the United States, Engen and Gale conclude that asset tests in other programs, such as those for college scholarships, "are deleterious to saving. While direct evidence is not available, one could extrapolate that similar effects would occur for Social Security" (1997, p. 129).

6.4   Conclusion

Examination of state pay-as-you-go pensions has elucidated the mechanism by which these pensions can displace private savings. Where people plan their savings over the life cycle, then the existence of state pensions is likely to reduce other forms of savings. Reduced savings leads—if endogenous growth theory is to be believed—to a lower rate of growth, or—in a neoclassical perspective—to a lower level of output. However, those advocating cuts in state pensions typically propose that they be replaced by means-tested "targeted" pensions. This alternative runs the risk of creating a savings trap, and the net effect on savings of such a switch in policy is unclear. The disincentive to saving implicit in means-tested pensions risks creating the very dependency that critics of the welfare state deplore.

7

Investment, Pension Funds, and the Capital Market

Many people are urging a shift from state pay-as-you-go pensions to mandatory private funded pension provision for old age. The funding aspect of this proposal has received the most attention, notably the transition period and the possible double burden borne by the transitional generation. Here it is the *private* nature of the funded pensions on which I concentrate, since I believe it has implications that are not always appreciated.

Mandatory private funded pensions could take the form of individual savings, but in many cases it is suggested that there are special private pension institutions. In order to meet the legislative requirements, or to qualify for a reduction in state contributions, private provision typically has to be in some protected form, either an occupational scheme or one operated by a pension institution such as a pension fund or life assurance company. Occupational schemes in turn may be employer operated or may involve schemes operated on behalf of the employer by pension funds or life companies.

One immediate implication of these pension institutions is that they generate an interest group that lobbies the government about the statutes under which they operate, about regulation (as I know from having served as a member of the Pension Law Review Committee), about fiscal concessions, about international dimensions, and so on. There will be scope for exercizing political influence along the lines discussed in chapter 5. As Hannah commented in the case of the United Kingdom occupational pensions, "the pension industry has become a power in the land" (1986, p. 64). Such political influence is not necessarily neutral as far as the rate of growth is concerned. According to Olson (1995), the development of narrow special interest groups causes a slowdown in growth rates, although this cannot be independent of the objectives that the groups pursue.

Leaving aside in this chapter the political economy of private pensions, the existence of pension institutions such as pension funds has implications for the working of the economy. These considerations are often ignored in the theoretical analysis of the switch from state to private pensions. Employer operated schemes may affect the financing of the company sector, since the employer is liable for any deficit. The assets and liabilities of pension schemes enter into the assessment of a firm's financial position; they are relevant to the risk of bankruptcy and to possible takeover. Risk is borne not just by the shareholders but also by employees, and, as argued by Arnott and Gersovitz (1980), the corporate financial structure and employment contract are interdependent. The existence of a company pension scheme may enter into the value placed on a job, as examined in the models of chapters 3 and 4.

Whether or not linked to employers, the existence of private pension funds has the further implication that they may affect the operation of the capital market. Pension institutions acquire substantial weight in the capital market, and again may influence the working of the company sector. We cannot simply suppose that a switch to private pension provision would be neutral as far as the capital market is concerned. This switch may have implications for the rate of growth. A situation where savings are in the hands of pension funds is different from one where they belong to individual savers. It is on this aspect that I focus here. However, in order to explore the implications, we need to enrich the treatment of the capital market in the model of economic growth.

7.1   Treatment of Investment in Growth Models

To examine the role of the capital market, we need to introduce the corporate sector explicitly into the analysis. Companies make decisions about employment, as we have already been considering, and about investment. Investment has to date played no independent part in our discussion of growth. In the previous chapter it was supposed that changes in savings were automatically translated into changes in investment—that investment could be carried out of an amount equal to the level of savings, without consideration of the underlying mechanism. The unsatisfactory aspect of this assumption was noted by Uzawa (1969), who argued that the aggregative behavior of investment had been neglected in neoclassical growth models. He went on to introduce an explicit investment motive for firms:

[I]t is assumed that the business firm plans the levels of employment and investment in order to maximise the present value of expected future net cash flows. The desired level of investment per unit of real capital will be shown to depend upon the expected rate of profit and the market rate of interest. (1969, p. 629)

Similarly, Eltis (1973), in his model of equilibrium growth, considers the choice of the firm between retaining profits and paying out dividends, and examines the implications of firms maximizing their share price. He derives an investment function such that the desired rate of growth of capital depends positively on the rate of profit and negatively on the rate of interest (see also, Eltis 1963).

In both formulations, a distinction is drawn between the rate of interest, here denoted i, and the rate of profit, denoted by r as before. This distinction is the first ingredient in the model considered here. The second ingredient is the link between personal and corporate sectors, building on the original introduction by Kaldor (1966) of equity share values into the capital accumulation equations. Where companies retain profits, then they are saving on behalf of the shareholders, and whether this is fully offset depends on the valuation ratio (the ratio of the stock market value of the firm to the value of its capital assets), as shown by Moore (1973, 1975). The decision by companies to retain profits is in part a financial one, where retained earnings may be substituted by issuing new debt or by new share issues, and in part a real decision, in that further retentions, other things equal, allow a higher level of investment. Here I focus on the real rather than the financial decision: by deciding to retain a larger proportion of its profits, a firm is deciding to increase its capital stock. In the next section I describe such a corporate growth model.

7.2   A Corporate Growth Model

In this section I bring together a simple model of corporate behavior with the AK theory of endogenous growth sketched in chapter 6. As suggested in Atkinson 1994, it may be useful to view the investment rate in an endogenous growth model as being governed by the choice of growth rate by firms that face costs of adjustment.[21] This marries two different literatures: that on the growth of the firm (initiated by Penrose 1959; Baumol 1962; Marris 1964) and that on endogenous growth theory. Such a proposal of marriage is not novel: it emerges from the work of Uzawa (1969) on the Penrose effect and of Odagiri (1981) on corporate growth, on both of which I have drawn significantly.

In order to make this more concrete, let us suppose that the firm has an initial scale, K, generating a gross profit per unit of capital, r. Moreover let us suppose that the investment, I, is financed entirely out of retained earnings with no new issues or debt finance. The only assets in the economy are shares. (In a fuller treatment, the financial decision needs to be incorporated taking account of the tax implications (Atkinson and Stiglitz 1980, lecture 5), which may have particular significance in an international context (Sinn 1987).

At any moment, a dividend per unit of capital is paid equal to that part of profit that is not invested:

$$r - I/K. \tag{7.1}$$

The value to the shareholders of this stream of dividends, which in steady state grows at rate g with the growth of K, is assumed to be the present discounted value at the rate of interest i. This means that the steady state value, v, of a share corresponding to one unit of capital today is:

$$v = (r - I/K)/(i - g). \tag{7.2}$$

This is the same as

$$iv = (r - I/K) + gv. \tag{7.3}$$

The right-hand side is the rate of return on equities, taking account of capital gains at rate g (in steady state the value of a share rises at exponential rate g), and this is equal to the interest rate, since there is no risk premium. (This is essentially the same formula as (3.12) but applied in a quite different context.)

The feature emphasized in the managerial models of Penrose, Marris, and others is that growth has costs. It is not simply a matter of buying new capital equipment. The work has to be managed; expansion takes up scarce time of executives; new staff have to be integrated into the team. Alternatively, there are costs of expanding sales: an investment in sales promotion is necessary if the firm is to grow at a faster rate (Solow 1971). This is represented here by the assumption that

$$I/K = c(g), \quad \text{where} \quad c'(g) > 0, c''(g) > 0, c'(0) = 1. \quad (7.4)$$

This cost of growth function is shown in figure 7.1, where there is assumed to be a maximum feasible growth rate, g_{max}. In other words, the marginal cost of increasing the growth rate is initially simply the cost of the investment (the slope at $g = 0$ is equal to 1), but at positive growth rates there is an additional cost (the curve lies below the 45° line in figure 7.1). It should be noted that this is internal growth and that no takeovers take place.

Combining (7.2) and (7.4), we can see that a firm that maximizes its share value chooses the growth rate to maximize

$$v = [r - c(g)]/(i - g). \quad (7.5)$$

The first-order condition for the choice of g is that

$$\partial v/\partial g = -c'(g)/(i - g) + [r - c(g)]/(i - g)^2 = 0 \quad (7.6)$$

or that

$$c'(g) = [r - c(g)]/(i - g). \quad (7.7)$$

The solution is depicted in figure 7.1, which is drawn on the assumption that

$$r > i > g_{max}. \quad (7.8)$$

The chosen growth rate is identified by taking a point A with coordinates (r, i), which by assumption is between the 45° line and the $c(g)$ curve, and locating the tangent from A to this

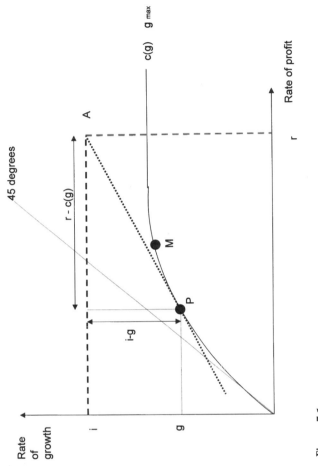

Figure 7.1
Choice of corporate growth rate to maximize share value

curve, at point P. It may be noted that the value of a share is given by the inverse of the slope of the tangent, since this latter is equal to $(i - g)/(r - c(g))$. (The first-order condition can be written as $c'(g) = v$). The maximized value is referred to later as v_{max}.

The rate of growth chosen by a firm that maximizes its stock market value is an increasing function of the rate of profit. A rise in r means that the point A in figure 7.1 moves horizontally to the right, and the new tangent on the $c(g)$ curve is above P. Equally, we can deduce that the rate of growth is a declining function of the rate of interest: a rise in i shifts the point A vertically upwards in figure 7.1, and the point of tangency shifts to the left. The chosen growth rate is depicted as a function of i (holding r constant) in figure 7.2 by the downward-sloping solid curve. The relevant region is where $i \geq g$. In the limit, as i approaches r, the chosen growth rate falls to zero.

Endogenous Growth

All of this is contained in the earlier literature, and cost of adjustment models are widespread in macroeconomics (e.g., Lucas 1967 or Abel and Blanchard 1983). What is new here is bringing the cost of adjustment investment function together with the simple learning by doing model outlined in chapter 6. The endogeneity of the growth rate is important, since it resolves an important difficulty identified in the earlier literature: reconciling the growth rate chosen by a representative firm with the natural growth rate of the economy. This difficulty was described by Solow as follows:

The whole economy is assumed to be growing at its natural rate, g_o. Obviously this creates a problem. If a firm should choose to grow forever at a rate g which is larger than g_o, eventually it (or whichever

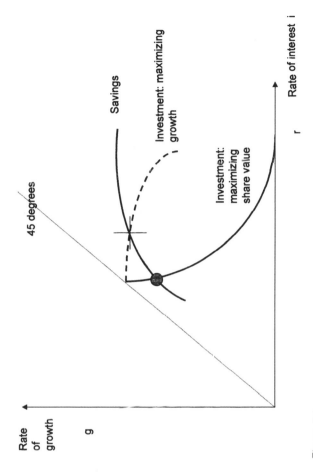

Figure 7.2
Equilibrium in corporate economy: Share value maximization and managerially controlled firm

firm chooses the largest rate of growth) must dominate the whole economy, and the economy will be growing not at g_o, but at g. (1971, pp. 319–20)

But one of the implications of the new growth theory is that there is *no* natural rate of growth. If firms collectively choose to grow faster, then in aggregate productivity rises faster through learning by doing. So the new growth theory is a natural background for the growth theories of the firm. This point was made by Odagiri (1981) in that he allowed firms to influence the rate of technical progress by allocating resources to research and development.

Equilibrium of savings and investment is achieved by variation in the rate of interest. Suppose that savings are governed by the two-period life cycle mechanism described in the previous chapter (switching to discrete time), so that, solving equations (6.12) and (6.14) for g, and replacing r with i (since household savings depend on the rate of interest, which is now i), we have

$$g = [\sigma - t + (1 - \sigma)ti/(1 + i) - 1/(a(1 - \beta))]/$$

$$[1/(a(1 - \beta)) + (1 - \sigma)t/(1 + i)]. \qquad (7.9)$$

This is shown by the upward-sloping savings curve in figure 7.2, where the relevant part is where $i \geq g$. Savings increase with the interest rate because a rise in i reduces the value of the state pension. In the absence of the pension, the savings rate would be independent of i, but this is a special property of the Cobb-Douglas form assumed for the utility function. The resulting equilibrium is shown in figure 7.2 by the dot.

In the theories of corporate growth, considerable emphasis was placed on an alternative hypothesis about firm behavior: that firms maximize the rate of growth subject to a takeover constraint. The constraint may take the form of limiting the stock market value to some fraction of the "breakup" value of the assets:

$$v \geq m. \tag{7.10}$$

The reasons why such a hypothesis has been examined are described by Baumol:

Economists who have spent time observing the operations of business enterprises come away impressed with the extent of management's occupation with growth.... Indeed, in talking to business executives one may easily come to believe that growth of the firm is the main preoccupation of top management. A stationary optimum would doubtless be abhorrent to the captains of industry, whose main concern is ... how rapidly to grow. (1962, p. 1078)

Of course, shareholders are aware of the principal-agent problem, and sale of their shares to a takeover bidder is not the only means by which they may seek to constrain managers to increase share values. They may not simply be passive in the face of agency costs. As Jensen and Meckling (1976) pointed out, shareholders have a variety of devices, including the direct monitoring discussed in the next section. However, even optimal monitoring and guarantees by the management will not ensure maximization of stock market value. Similarly, stock option and profit-related remuneration schemes are incentives to managers to put aside their own interests, but as we have seen in chapter 5, imperfect information means that even the best designed incentive scheme may allow some latitude to managers.[22]

In the managerial case, managers choose the highest rate of growth consistent with the takeover constraint: that is,

$$v = [r - c(g)]/(i - g) \geq m. \tag{7.11}$$

On the assumption that this constraint is not binding at the previously chosen growth rate P in figure 7.1, we can see that the growth maximizing firm will choose the point M above P where the inverse of the slope of MA is equal to m. This yields a higher rate of growth at any interest rate. Transposed to figure 7.2, the investment behavior of the firm is shown by the curve IM. There is a new equilibrium with a higher growth rate (and interest rate). This is shown in figure 7.2 by the intersection, marked by a cross, of the savings curve with the dashed investment curve.

7.3   Capital Markets and Private Pensions

The elaboration of the capital market model allows us to investigate the impact of a move from state to private pensions, where the latter are invested in private pension funds. The first effect is an upward shift in the savings function, as analyzed above. This tends to raise the equilibrium rate of growth for both profit maximizing and growth maximizing firms.

There is, however, a second possible effect. As already noted, private pension funds come to play a more important role in the capital market. In the case of Sweden, such a development is welcomed by the Lindbeck Commission: "It is also important to stimulate the emergence of a larger number of institutions that not only hold shares, but are also willing to play an active ownership role" (Lindbeck et al. 1994, p. 96). The potential impact of pension funds on the capital market is recognized by the World Bank (1994) in its report *Averting the Old Age Crisis*. They note that institutionalizing savings may make it harder for small firms and new ventures to obtain financing. But in the case of larger corporations, they view the growth of pension funds as beneficial: "when pension funds have a big stake in corporate equities, they are in a better position than individuals to overcome 'free rider' problems, demand improved accounting and auditing procedures, and get information. They are also better able to use that information to assess company managers and press for changes if management is not performing effectively" (World Bank, 1994, p. 177). They argue that when pension funds have only small stakes in companies they will fail to monitor managerial performance, but that as holdings increase so will pension funds increase their involvement in corporate governance.

These arguments take for granted that increased monitoring of companies moves their performance in a desired direction. On the other hand, if faster growth is regarded as desirable, then increased involvement by pension funds may have the reverse effect, as may be seen from the model outlined earlier. The precise nature of the takeover constraint (7.10) has not been spelled out, but there is good reason to expect that the larger the fraction of shares owned by pension funds, the tighter is likely to be the constraint.

In order to see the impact of greater institutional ownership, let us formalize the monitoring activity by shareholders. The behavior of the agent is parallel to the supply of effort by workers in the efficiency wage story (chapter 4), the difference being that "shirking" by managers involves choosing a higher growth rate than that which maximizes the share value, v. Suppose that corporate managers maximize the expected growth rate. The risk they face is that they will attract the attention of shareholders, which I assume will happen with a probability $\lambda(g)$ that is zero if the firm maximizes v (i.e., $v = v_{max}$) and a maximum λ^* if v were to fall to zero, where λ^* is a measure of the monitoring effort of shareholders:

$$\lambda(g) = \lambda^*[1 - v(g)/v_{max}]. \tag{7.12}$$

If the investors find that v is less than v_{max}, then there will be a takeover bid, in which case the return to the management is zero (they lose their position). The payoff for the managers is

g with probability $(1 - \lambda(g))$ and zero with probability $\lambda(g)$, yielding an expected payoff of $(1 - \lambda(g))g$.

The risk to managers of a takeover increases with g (since v is a decreasing function of g above the optimum). Maximizing the expected managerial payoff yields the first-order condition:

$$g(-\partial v/\partial g) = v + v_{max}(1/\lambda^* - 1).\tag{7.13}$$

The right-hand side is clearly a decreasing function of λ^*. (See figure 7.3 for a graphical version of the managers' choice.) The greater the degree of monitoring, the closer the chosen growth rate to that which maximizes the share value.

The gain from monitoring is that the share value increases from $v(g)$, the value chosen by the "shirking" managers, to v_{max}, the maximum value. Monitoring has costs, and small investors will not incur these costs, preferring to free-ride on the activities of others. A pension fund that owns a significant fraction, θ, of total equity may, however, find monitoring repays the cost, where these are taken to be $\mu(\lambda^*)$ and μ is an increasing convex function. The expected return net of monitoring costs is

$$\theta[v_{max} - v]\lambda^*[1 - v/v_{max}] - \mu(\lambda^*).\tag{7.14}$$

If the funds take the firms' choice of g as given, then they will maximize the expected net benefit where

$$\theta[v_{max} - v]^2/v_{max} = \mu'(\lambda^*).\tag{7.15}$$

The reaction of firms to an increase in monitoring means that the left-hand side is a declining function of λ^*, whereas the right-hand side is an increasing function.

It follows that an increase in the share of equity owned by pension funds leads to increased monitoring on their part, which increases the risk of takeover bids. Managers respond by reducing their chosen rate of growth, and hence there is a

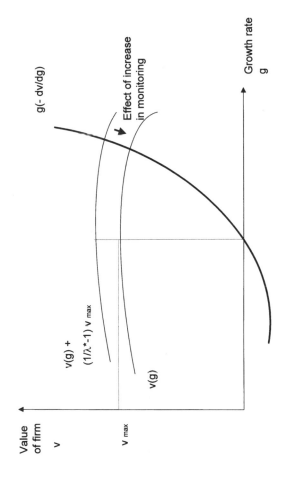

Figure 7.3
Monitoring by shareholders and risk of takeover

rise in v towards its maximum attainable value.[23] From figure 7.2, we can see that there is an inward shift in the IM curve (it rotates clockwise around the point where $i = g$). This is shown in detail in figure 7.4, where the initial position is marked by a cross. A switch in pension from unfunded state to funded private may lead to a rise in the savings rate but a fall in the desired growth rate of managerially controlled firms. The net effect may be to either raise or lower the rate of growth.

The takeover risk story is only one of many different representations of the firm growth decision. For example, in a model similar to that outlined here, Aoki (1980, 1982) has treated the growth of firms as determined by bargaining between shareholders and employees. Employees are concerned with the share of value added received, and only with growth insofar as this leads to rising remuneration over time. It is not therefore surprising that a shift in bargaining power toward shareholders in the Aoki model leads to a rise in the rate of growth (1982, p. 1104), although he notes that employees may press for higher markups (as in worker cooperatives) and that this may increase the attractiveness of growth (1980, p. 609), so that on this account a rise in shareholder power may reduce the chosen growth rate in certain circumstances.

The theoretical considerations I have discussed may appear remote from reality, but they echo the concerns of practical commentators. The World Bank proposals have been criticized as overstating the link between pension reform and faster economic growth, as in the study of Singh (1995), with particular reference to the experience of Chile. In the United States the growth in pension fund holdings has been much discussed: pension plan holdings of equities rose from 2 percent in 1955 to 23 percent in 1983 (Ippolito 1986, table 9-2). The growth of pension fund holdings in the United Kingdom over the past thirty years is shown in figure 7.5. In both countries there has

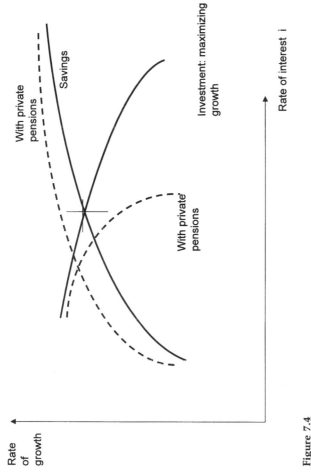

Figure 7.4
Effect of switch to private funded pensions where investment determined by managerially controlled firm

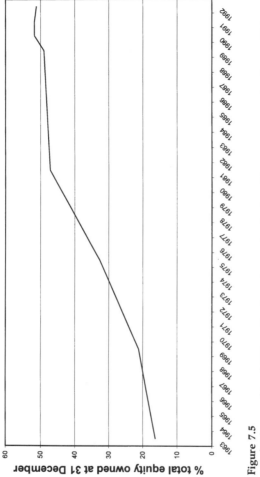

Figure 7.5
Beneficial ownership of U.K. equity shares by pension funds and insurance companies. Source: Hofmann and Lambert 1993, table 1.

been considerable concern about the short-term influence of financial institutions on investment decisions. The Goode Committee in the United Kingdom noted that there had been "widespread discussion of the 'short-termism' of pension funds. Those who identified this as a problem saw it as making long-term investment decisions in research and development or capital projects impossible for company managements to pursue" (Goode 1993, p. 159).

The empirical evidence on short-termism is mixed. Nickell summarizes the position as follows:

[T]here is very little evidence which conflicts with the existence of some degree of managerial myopia, particularly [where there is] pressure from the capital market which leads them to place the current share price and current earnings high on their list of objectives. . . . particularly in circumstances where there are large institutional shareholders whose fund-managers are judged on short-term results. (1995, p. 32)

Moreover, as the Goode Committee pointed out,

Perhaps it did not matter whether the institutions were 'short-termist' or not; the critical question was whether it changed the behaviour of company management to the detriment of the long-term prospects of the economy as a consequence of the mere belief that institutions were likely to behave in this manner. (1993, p. 159)

Bond, Chennells, and Devereux (1995) have drawn attention to the more than doubling of the dividend payout ratio in the United Kingdom since the 1970s, arguing that it is in part due to pressure from institutional investors like pension funds and that it may endanger business investment.

7.4 Conclusion

The aspect of pensions examined in this chapter is only one of the considerations that should enter the determination of policy, but it is one that has been neglected in the economic literature. The implications for economic performance of pension funds becoming a major actor in the capital market is widely assumed to be beneficial. In order to explore whether this is so, viewed in terms of increasing the rate of growth, the endogenous growth model used in chapter 6 has been extended to allow explicitly for the independent role of investment decisions, which the noneconomist might expect to be to the fore in any theory of economic growth. Where there is a separation of ownership and control in making such decisions, corporate managers may be interested in raising the growth rate at the expense of maximizing share valuation. If increased ownership of shares by private pension funds leads to increased monitoring, and the interests of private pension funds are more in maximizing share values than in long-term growth, then the switch from state to private pensions may lower the growth rate. Whether or not this is desirable depends on the specification of social objectives. It could well be that a slower rate of growth is to be preferred; here I have concentrated simply on the question whether or not growth would be reduced.

8   Conclusions

Serious charges have been leveled at the welfare state, and they have to be taken seriously. If social transfer programs are indeed one of the major factors causing the present economic problems of OECD countries, then policy recommendations to scale back spending cannot be dismissed out of hand. Social, demographic, and labor market changes may have called into question the economic feasibility of the welfare state. At the same time, to reduce welfare state spending by amounts like 2 percent of GDP could have major implications for family living standards. The effectiveness of the welfare state in achieving its redistributional objectives is certainly open to criticism (and my first book, Atkinson 1969, was such a critique), but there can be little doubt about its importance in providing income support. There are major equity gains. Put bluntly, the rolling back of benefit coverage or reductions in benefit levels could hit hard some of the most disadvantaged members of our societies. Rolling back is not therefore to be undertaken lightly. Like much of the economic literature on the welfare state, I have concentrated in this book on its impact on economic performance to the neglect of the functions that the welfare state is intended to perform, but any final decision about welfare state policy requires us to look at both sides of the balance sheet. The economic costs are relevant, but so too are the benefits in terms of social objectives. Welfare state programs were introduced to meet certain goals, and one has to ask how far these goals could be achieved if a program were cut or eliminated.

The aim of this book has been to examine the basis for the claim that rolling back the welfare state would improve economic performance. As I stressed at the outset, my view of the problem is colored by being a citizen of a country whose experience has been special in a number of respects. It may well be that what appears to be true for the United Kingdom is not applicable to other OECD countries. Policy reforms appropriate to one country, say Sweden, may be irrelevant or damaging in another, say the United Kingdom. At the same time we are interdependent. Membership of the European Union implies that Sweden and the United Kingdom must have an eye to each other's policies. The title of Assar Lindbeck's painting on the cover of his book *The Swedish Experiment* (Lindbeck 1997) is "In the same boat."

The main conclusions I have drawn are summarized below:

Aggregate Empirical Evidence
The studies of the aggregate relationship between economic performance and the size of the welfare state reviewed here do not yield conclusive evidence. The results of econometric studies of the relationship between social transfer spending and growth rates are mixed: some find that high spending on social transfers leads to lower growth, others find the reverse. The largest of the estimated effects—in either direction—do not, however, seem believable.

Need for Theoretical Framework
To understand the connection between the welfare state and economic performance, the theoretical framework needs to be

set out explicitly. We cannot treat the relationship simply as a "black box." There are many mechanisms by which social transfers, and possible reforms, may affect the working of the economy. We need to investigate the underlying micro-economic relationships.

Distinguishing Different Questions

The theoretical framework helps clarify a number of important ambiguities in the charges, including:

• Are we concerned with GDP or with economic welfare? The welfare state may increase output but distort individual choices. Which should be the principal object of our attention?

• Is it the level of GDP that is affected or its rate of growth? Is the charge that a large welfare state reduces the output of a country relative to that of others? Or does it cause it to grow more slowly, falling progressively further behind?

• Is the effect due to the tax burden of financing the welfare state? Or is it specific features of welfare state spending that damage economic performance? In this book, I have focused more on the specific features of the spending (for example, cutting unemployment insurance while holding tax rates constant) in order to separate the issues from those that arise as a result of the general fiscal problems of OECD countries.

Investigating Individual Transfer Programs

To assess the impact of the welfare state, we need to look at individual programs, since they have different economic implications. Here I have looked primarily at unemployment insurance and state pay-as-you-go pensions. These are two of the most controversial programs, but it must be remembered that other types of spending may raise different issues.

Importance of Institutional Structure

An important role is played by the institutional structure of the welfare state. The form of benefits, and the conditions under which they may be claimed, can change their impact on economic behavior. The same level of total spending may have different implications for the level of GDP or the long-run growth rate, depending on the entitlement structure. Transfer programs may have positive or negative economic consequences, depending on how they are structured.

Unemployment Insurance

Examination of unemployment insurance, taking account of the way it is administered, shows that the effects are potentially more subtle than often supposed. It is true that the existence of benefit may make people more likely to queue for jobs in the high wage sector, but they may also lower the wage premium in that sector. The disqualification conditions of unemployment insurance mean that it reinforces, rather than undermines, the nonshirking condition in the secondary sector. Cutting benefit levels, or reducing their coverage, may lead unions to seek to restore wage differentials, and secondary employers may have to pay a higher efficiency wage, with adverse effects on employment.

State Pensions

Examination of state pay-as-you-go pensions has elucidated the mechanism by which these pensions displace private savings. Reduced savings leads—if endogenous growth theory is to be believed—to a lower rate of growth or—in a neoclassical perspective—to a lower level of output. It is, however, important to ask what would replace state pensions. Most people have in mind that there would continue to be a means-tested safety net. Such a safety net may, however, create a savings trap, where a fraction of the population have no incentive to save for their old age. For the non-means-tested tier, it is envisaged that state provision be replaced by private funded pensions, but this would have implications for the capital market. Pension fund managers are, paradoxically, short-term in their horizons. Firms on the equity market may find that they are constrained to invest less and grow more slowly than their managers would otherwise choose. Switching to "targeted" benefits or to private provision may therefore replace one set of disincentives with another.

Political Economy of the Welfare State

The future of the welfare state is a highly political issue. In seeking to understand the determinants of spending on social transfers, we need to consider the political mechanisms in operation. Pressures to scale back the welfare state may reflect a shift in voter preferences, either exogenous or endogenous, where there has been a "lifting of the veil" following the rise in unemployment. If there is political slack, then the explanation may be found in politician's preferences and in the objectives of civil servants. It may be that there has been a shift in the balance of administrative power, with agencies acquiring greater power and civil servants less, or there may be reduced political influence exercised by pressure groups representing beneficiaries. The dynamics of the welfare state may have been fundamentally changed by the alarms raised about the feasibility of its continuance. Calls by economists for rolling back the welfare state are themselves part of the political process; we have not just endogenous politicians but also endogenous economists, whose behavior has to be explained.

Notes

1. I share the distaste for this term expressed by Vickrey, who described it as "one of the most vicious euphemisms ever coined" (1993, p. 2).

2. There is a profusion of statistics comparing social transfer spending in different countries. The figures in figures 2.1 and 2.2 are from the OECD Historical Statistics and relate only to social security transfers, excluding other government transfer payments. They are broadly similar to the figures for "cash benefits" published by the ILO in *The Cost of Social Security* (1992). On the other hand, the figures in figures 2.1 and 2.2 differ from the statistics for income transfers also produced by the OECD (see, for example, Barr 1994, Tables 1–3), which include, in the case of the United Kingdom, payments under private occupational pension schemes. The figures in figures 2.1 and 2.2 differ also from those for social protection expenditure published by Eurostat (for example, European Commission 1993, p. 42), which include benefits in kind and expenditure on public health services.

3. Factors that need to be taken into account include the growth in the number of recipients, which is examined in detail by Le Grand and colleagues (see Barr and Coulter 1990).

4. This is not an exhaustive list of such studies. Just to give one example of a study that came to my attention after the appendix was completed, see Lane and Ersson (1985).

5. Two reviews in Swedish that reach rather different conclusions are Söderström 1994 and Agell, Lindh, and Ohlsson 1994. I owe these references to Klevmarken 1994. See also Agell, Lindh, and Ohlsson 1995, and the Controversy in the *Economic Journal*: Korpi (1996), Henrekson (1996), Agell (1996), and Dowrick (1996).

6. Reference should also be made to Levine and Renelt 1992, who find that the estimated relationships with GDP growth of total government expenditure and government consumption to be "fragile."

7. Hansson and Henrekson (1994), for example, find a significant negative co-efficient on total transfers but a smaller and less significant coefficient for social security alone. Since total transfers include subsidies to firms and interest payments on the national debt, this seems a less relevant variable for the present purpose.

8. A study framed in this way, and not included in table 2.1, is that by Friedland and Sanders (1985), which in a twelve country analysis for the period 1962–1983 finds a positive association between growth rates and increases in the ratio to GDP of government transfer payments to households.

9. McCallum and Blais (1987) adjust total social security spending to allow for differences between countries in the proportion of population aged 65 and over.

10. There is an obvious link with evolutionary game theory. Among the many references are Axelrod 1984, Sugden 1989, Young 1990, and Bicchieri, Jeffrey, and Skyrms 1997.

11. There may also be arguments along these lines against active labour market programs (as examined, for example, by Calmfors 1995 and Calmfors and Lang 1995) or against public employment programs (see Holmlund and Lindén 1993), but I focus here on cash transfers.

12. I concentrate on unemployment benefits paid as a flow during a period of unemployment; the model could also be used to examine the implications of redundancy payments paid as a lump sum to workers whose jobs are terminated. Such turnover costs are examined by, among others, Bertola 1990, Bentolila and Bertola 1990, Bertola 1992, Bertola and Ichino 1995, Carling et al. 1995, and Saint-Paul 1996.

13. For further comparative information on unemployment insurance in Europe, see, among others, Brunhes and Annandale-Massa 1986 and Schmid, Reissert, and Bruche 1992.

14. In the United Kingdom, the National Association of Citizens Advice Bureaux commented as follows on the severity of disqualification from unemployment benefit: "The practice of automatically suspending the payment of benefits while claims are under investigation, the delays in reaching decisions on claims and the duration and severity of the financial penalties imposed following disqualification leave many claimants facing financial hardship which is out of all proportion to the original purpose" (1994, p. 2).

15. For discussion of union negotiated unemployment benefits, see Oswald (1986), Holmlund and Lundborg (1988), and Kiander (1993).

16. As has been pointed out to me by Agnar Sandmo, there is a parallel with the irreversibility identified by Johansen (1982) in his treatment of employment and unemployment with heterogenous labor: workers not laid off in a recession learn their value to the employer, and employers are less willing to take on the unemployed in the next upswing.

17. A different dynamic story is that of Matzner (1996), who argues, in a game-theoretic treatment, that for Western societies the implosion of the Soviet Union led to a change from cooperative behavior with a positive sum outcome to noncooperative behavior with a zero or negative sum outcome.

18. The comparative statics of pressure group activity are discussed further in Kristov, Lindert, and McClelland 1992.

19. Beginning with the work of Romer (1986) and Lucas (1988). Recent textbook accounts are given by Barro and Sala-i-Martin (1995), Romer (1996), and Aghion and Howitt (1998).

20. For textbook treatments of this model, see Atkinson and Stiglitz 1980, (section 8.4) and Romer 1996 (chapter 2, part B). A rather different version of the life-cycle model has been set out by Blanchard (1985), where there is a constant probability of death, and wages decline exponentially over the lifetime. This has been used by Saint-Paul (1992) to argue that an unfunded social security system reduces the growth rate.

21. Two recent studies of growth with adjustment costs are Turnovsky 1996 and Ploeg 1996.

22. For a discussion of the effect of stock option and other schemes on managerially controlled firms, see Scott 1989, section 9.12.

23. Empirical evidence in the United States, as summarized by Mayer, finds that "corporate performance [v] initially rises with low levels of concentration of ownership (for example, up to 5% ...) and then declines" (1996, p. 8).

References

Aaron, H. 1966. "The Social Insurance Paradox." *Canadian Journal of Economics and Political Science* 32: 371–374.

Aaron, H. 1967. "Social Security: International Comparisons." In *Studies in the Economics of Income Maintenance*, ed. O. Eckstein. Washington, D.C.: Brookings Institution, pp. 13–48.

Abel, A. B., and O. J. Blanchard. 1983. "An Intertemporal Model of Saving and Investment." *Econometrica* 51: 675–692.

Abramovitz, M. 1981. "Welfare Quandaries and Productivity Concerns." *American Economic Review* 71: 1–17.

Agell, J., 1996. "Why Sweden's Welfare State Needed Reform." *Economic Journal* 106: 1760–1771.

Agell, J., T. Lindh, and H. Ohlsson. 1994. "Tillväxt och offentlig sektor." *Ekonomisk Debatt* 22: 373–385.

Agell, J., T. Lindh, and H. Ohlsson. 1995. "Growth and the Public Sector: A Critical Review Essay." Working paper 1995: 9, Department of Economics, Uppsala University.

Aghion, P. and P. Howitt. 1998. *Endogenous Growth Theory*. Cambridge, MA: MIT Press.

Akerlof, G. A. 1982. "Labor Contracts as Partial Gift Exchange." *Quarterly Journal of Economics* 97: 543–569.

Akerlof, G. A. 1984. "Gift Exchange and Efficiency Wage Theory: Four Views." *American Economic Review*, Papers and Proceedings 74: 79–83.

Akerlof, G. A. and J. Yellen, eds. 1986. *Efficiency Wage Models of the Labour Market*. Cambridge: Cambridge University Press.

Albrecht, J. W. and B. Axell. 1984. "An Equilibrium Model of Search Unemployment." *Journal of Political Economy* 92: 824–840.

Albrecht, J. W., B. Axell, and H. Lang. 1986. "General Equilibrium Wage and Price Distributions." *Quarterly Journal of Economics* 101: 687–706.

Aoki, M. 1980. "A Model of the Firm as a Stockholder-Employee Cooperative Game." *American Economic Review* 70: 600–610.

Aoki, M. 1982. "Equilibrium Growth of the Hierarchical Firm." *American Economic Review* 72: 1097–1110.

Armstrong, M., S. Cowan, and J. Vickers. 1994. *Regulatory Reform*. Cambridge, MA: MIT Press.

Arnott, R. J. and M. Gersovitz. 1980. "Corporate Financial Structure and the Funding of Private Pension Plans." *Journal of Public Economics* 13: 231–247.

Arrow, K. J. 1962. "The Economic Implications of Learning by Doing." *Review of Economic Studies* 29: 155–173.

Atkinson, A. B. 1969. *Poverty in Britain and the Reform of Social Security*. Cambridge: Cambridge University Press.

Atkinson, A. B. 1989. *Poverty and Social Security*. Hemel Hempstead: Harvester.

Atkinson, A. B. 1990. "Income Maintenance for the Unemployed in Britain and the Response to High Unemployment." *Ethics* 100: 569–585. Reprinted as chapter 9 in Atkinson 1996.

Atkinson, A. B. 1991. "Social Insurance." *Geneva Papers on Risk and Insurance Theory* 16: 113–131. Reprinted as chapter 11 in Atkinson 1996.

Atkinson, A. B. 1992a. "Institutional Features of Unemployment Insurance and the Working of the Labour market." In *Economic Analysis of Markets and Games*, eds. P. Dasgupta, D. Gale, E. Maskin, and O. Hart Cambridge, MA: MIT Press, pp. 82–106. Reprinted as chapter 10 in Atkinson 1996.

Atkinson, A. B. 1992b. "Towards a European Social Safety Net?" *Fiscal Studies* 13: 41–53. Reprinted as chapter 14 in Atkinson 1996.

Atkinson, A. B. 1994. "What has Happened to the Macro-economic Theory of Distribution?" Caffè Lectures, University of Rome La Sapienza.

Atkinson, A. B. 1995. "The Welfare State and Economic Performance." *National Tax Journal* 48: 171–198.

Atkinson, A. B. 1996. *Incomes and the Welfare State*. Cambridge: Cambridge University Press.

Atkinson, A. B. and J. Micklewright. 1989. "Turning the Screw: Benefits for the Unemployed 1979–88." In *The Economics of Social Security*, eds. A. Dilnot and I. Walker. Oxford: Oxford University Press, pp. 17–51. Reprinted as chapter 8 in Atkinson 1989.

Atkinson, A. B. and J. Micklewright. 1991. "Unemployment Compensation and Labor Market Transitions: A Critical Review." *Journal of Economic Literature* 29: 1679–1727.

Atkinson, A. B. and J. E. Stiglitz. 1980. *Lectures on Public Economics*. New York: McGraw-Hill.

Axell, B. and H. Lang. 1990. "The Effects of Unemployment Compensation in General Equilibrium with Search Unemployment." *Scandinavian Journal of Economics* 92: 531–540.

Axelrod, R. 1984. *The Evolution of Cooperation*. New York: Basic Books.

Barr, N. 1988. "The Mirage of Private Unemployment Insurance." Welfare State Programme Discussion Paper, London School of Economics.

Barr, N. 1992. "Economic Theory and the Welfare State: A Survey and Interpretation." *Journal of Economic Literature* 30: 741–803.

Barr, N. 1994. *Labor Markets and Social Policy in Central and Eastern Europe*. Oxford: Oxford University Press.

Barr, N. and F. Coulter. 1990. "Social Security: Solution or Problem?" In J. Hills, *The State of Welfare*. Oxford: Clarendon Press.

Barro, R. J. 1991. "Economic Growth in a Cross Section of Countries." *Quarterly Journal of Economics* 106: 407–443.

Barro, R. J. 1997. *Determinants of Economic Growth*. Cambridge, MA: MIT Press.

Barro, R. J. and X. Sala-i-Martin. 1995. *Economic Growth*. New York: McGraw-Hill.

Baumol, W. J. 1962. "On the Theory of the Expansion of the Firm." *American Economic Review* 52: 1078–1087.

Bean, C. R. 1994. "European Unemployment: A Survey." *Journal of Economic Literature* 32: 573–619.

Becker, G. S. 1983. "A Theory of Competition Among Pressure Groups for Political Influence." *Quarterly Journal of Economics* 98: 371–400.

Becker, G. S. 1985. "Public Policies, Pressure Groups, and Dead Weight Costs." *Journal of Public Economics* 28: 329–347.

Bentolila, S. and G. Bertola. 1990. "Firing Costs and Labor Demand." *Review of Economics Studies* 57: 381–402.

Bertola, G. 1990. "Job Security, Employment and Wages." *European Economic Review* 34: 851–886.

Bertola, G. 1992. "Labor Turnover Costs and Average Labor Demand." *Journal of Labor Economics* 10: 389–411.

Bertola, G. 1993. "Factor Shares and Savings in Endogenous Growth." *American Economic Review* 83: 1184–1198.

Bertola, G. and A. Ichino. 1995. "Wage Inequality and Unemployment: U.S. vs. Europe." *NBER Macroeconomics Annual* 10: 13–54.

Beveridge, Sir William (later Lord). 1942. *Social Insurance and Allied Services.* London: HMSO.

Beveridge, Sir William (later Lord). 1944. *Full Employment in a Free Society.* London: Allen and Unwin.

Bicchieri, C., R. Jeffrey, and B. Skyrms. 1997. *The Dynamics of Norms.* Cambridge: Cambridge University Press.

Bird, E. J. 1998. "Does the Welfare State Induce Risk Taking?" Working Paper no. 12, Wallis Institute of Political Economy, University of Rochester.

Blanchard, O. 1985. "Debts, Deficits, and Finite Horizons." *Journal of Political Economy* 93: 223–247.

Blanchard, O. and P. A. Diamond. 1990. "The Aggregate Matching Function." In *Growth, Productivity, Unemployment,* ed. P. A. Diamond. Cambridge, MA: MIT Press, pp. 159–201.

Blank, R. M. and D. E. Card. 1991. "Recent Trends in Insured and Uninsured Unemployment: Is There an Explanation?" *Quarterly Journal of Economics* 106: 1157–1190.

Bond, S. R., L. Chennells, and M. P. Devereux. 1995. "Taxes and Company Dividends: A Microeconometric Investigation Exploiting Cross-section Variation in Taxes." Institute for Fiscal Studies Working Paper 95/11.

Booth, A. L. 1995. *The Economics of the Trade Union.* Cambridge: Cambridge University Press.

Brennan, G. and J. M. Buchanan. 1977. "Towards a Tax Constitution for Leviathan." *Journal of Public Economics* 8: 255–274.

Brennan, G. and J. M. Buchanan. 1978. "Tax Instruments as Constraints on the Disposition of Public Revenues." *Journal of Public Economics* 9: 301–318.

Brunhes, B. and D. Annandale-Massa. 1986. *L'Indemnisation du Chômage en Europe*. Paris: L'UNEDIC.

Bulow, J. I. and L. H. Summers. 1986. "A Theory of Dual Labor Markets with Application to Industrial Policy, Discrimination, and Keynesian Unemployment." *Journal of Labor Economics* 4: 376–414.

Calmfors, L. 1995. "Labour Market Policy and Unemployment." *European Economic Review* 39: 583–592.

Calmfors, L. and H. Lang. 1995. "Macroeconomic Effects of Active Labour Market Programmes in a Union Wage-Setting Model." *Economic Journal* 105: 601–619.

Carling, K., P.-A. Edin, A. Harkman, and B. Holmlund. 1995. "Unemployment Duration, Unemployment Benefits, and Labour Market Programmes in Sweden." CEPR Discussion Paper 1200.

Castles, F. G. and S. Dowrick. 1990. "The Impact of Government Spending Levels on Medium-Term Economic Growth in the OECD, 1960–85." *Journal of Theoretical Politics* 2: 173–204.

Coates, K. and R. Silburn. 1970. *Poverty: the Forgotten Englishmen*. London: Penguin.

Collins, J. 1993. "Occupational Pensions for the Less Well Off: Who Benefits?" *Watsons Quarterly* no. 28: 4–7.

Crosland, C. A. R. 1956. *The Future of Socialism*. London: Cape.

Danziger, S., R. Haveman, and R. Plotnick. 1981. "How Income Transfer Programs Affect Work, Savings and the Income Distribution: A Critical Review." *Journal of Economic Literature* 19: 975–1028.

Davidson, C. and S. A. Woodbury. 1997. "Optimal Unemployment Insurance." *Journal of Public Economics* 64: 359–387.

Denison, E. F. 1962. "Sources of Growth in the United States and the Alternatives Before Us." Supplement Paper 13, Committee for Economic Development, New York.

Denison, E. F. 1967. *Why Growth Rates Differ*. Washington, D.C.: Brookings Institution.

Diamond, P. A. 1965. "National Debt in a Neoclassical Growth Model." *American Economic Review* 55: 1126–1150.

Diamond, P. A. 1981. "Mobility Costs, Frictional Unemployment, and Efficiency." *Journal of Political Economy* 89: 798–812.

Diamond, P. A. 1993. "Insulation of Pensions from Political Risk." Conference on Mandatory Pensions, Santiago, Chile (January 1994).

Diamond, P. A. 1996. "Proposals to Restructure Social Security." *Journal of Economic Perspectives* 10, no. 3: 67–88.

Diamond, P. A. 1997. "Macroeconomic Aspects of Social Security Reform." *Brookings Papers on Economic Activity*, no. 2: 1–66.

Dickens, W. T. 1994. Discussion of Gottschalk, P and Moffitt, R, "The Growth of Earnings Instability in the U.S. Labor Market", *Brookings Papers on Economic Activity*. no. 2: 217–272.

Disney, R. 1982. "Theorising the Welfare State: the Case of Unemployment Insurance." *Journal of Social Policy* 11: 35–58.

Dixit, A. K. 1996. *The Making of Economic Policy*. Cambridge, MA: MIT Press.

Doeringer, P. B. and M. J. Piore. 1971. *Internal Labor Markets and Manpower Analysis*. Lexington, MA: D.C. Heath.

Dowrick, S. 1996. "Swedish Economic Performance and Swedish Economic Debate: A View from Outside." *Economic Journal* 106: 1747–1759.

Drèze, J. H. and E. Malinvaud. 1994. "Growth and Employment: The Scope for a European Initiative." *European Economy* no. 1: 77–106.

Elmeskov, J. 1993. "High and Persistent Unemployment: Assessment of the Problem and its Causes." OECD Economics Department Working Paper 132, OECD, Paris.

Eltis, W. A. 1963. "Investment, Technical Progress, and Economic Growth." *Oxford Economic Papers* 15: 32–52.

Eltis, W. A. 1973. *Growth and Distribution*. London: Macmillan.

Engen, E. M. and Gale, W. G. 1997. "Effects of Social Security Reform on Private and National Saving." In *Social Security Reform*, eds. S. A. Sass and R. K. Triest. Federal Reserve Bank of Boston Conference Series No. 41, Boston pp. 103–142.

Englander, A. S. and A. Gurney. 1994. "Medium-Term Determinants of OECD Productivity." *OECD Economic Studies*, no. 22: 49–109.

European Commission. 1993. *Social Protection in Europe*. Brussels: European Commission.

European Commission. 1994. *MISSOC—Social Protection in the Member States of the Union—Situation on July 1st 1993*. Brussels: Official Publications of the European Communities.

European Commission. 1995. *MISSOC—Social Protection in the Member States of the Union—Situation on 1 July 1994*. Brussels: Official Publications of the European Communities.

European Commission. 1996. *MISSOC—Social Protection in the Member States of the Union—Situation on 1 July 1995*. Brussels: Official Publications of the European Communities.

European Commission. 1997. *MISSOC—Social Protection in the Member States of the Union—Situation on 1 July 1996*. Brussels: Official Publications of the European Communities.

Feldstein, M. S. 1974. "Social Security, Induced Retirement and Aggregate Capital Accumulation." *Journal of Political Economy* 82: 905–926.

Feldstein, M. S. 1976a. "Social Security and Saving: The Extended Life Cycle Theory." *American Economic Review* 66: 76–86.

Feldstein, M. S. 1976b. "Temporary Layoffs in the Theory of Unemployment." *Journal of Political Economy* 84: 937–957.

Feldstein, M. S. 1987. "Should Social Security Benefits Be Means Tested?" *Journal of Political Economy* 95: 468–484.

Feldstein, M. S. 1996. "The Missing Piece in Policy Analysis: Social Security Reform." *American Economic Review*, Papers and Proceedings 86: 1–14.

Finn, D. 1996. "The Job Seeker's Allowance Won't Help the Unemployed." *New Economy* 3: 60–65.

Franco, D. and T. Munzi. 1996. "Public Pension Expenditure Prospects in the European Union: A Survey of National Projections." *European Economy*, no. 3: 1–126.

Freeman, R. 1995. "The Large Welfare State as a System." *American Economic Review*, Papers and Proceedings 85: 16–21.

Freeman, R., B. Swedenborg, and R. Topel, eds. 1997. *Reforming the Welfare State: The Swedish Model in Transition*. Chicago: Chicago University Press.

Friedland, R. and J. Sanders. 1985. "The Public Economy and Economic Growth in Western Market Economies." *American Sociological Review* 50: 421–437.

Garraty, J. A. 1978. *Unemployment in History*. New York: Harper.

Gilbert, N. and A. Moon. 1988. "Analyzing Welfare Effort: An Appraisal of Comparative Methods." *Journal of Policy Analysis and Management* 7: 326–340.

Goode, R. (chairman). 1993. *Pension Law Reform*. London: HMSO.

Goodin, R. E. and J. Dryzek. 1987. "Risk Sharing and Social Justice: The Motivational Foundations of the Post-War Welfare State." In *Not Only the Poor*, eds. R. E. Goodin and J. Le Grand. London: Allen and Unwin, pp. 37–73.

Gottschalk, P. and R. Moffitt. 1994. "The Growth of Earnings Instability in the U.S. Labor Market." *Brookings Papers on Economic Activity*, no. 2: 217–272.

Gramlich, E. M. 1996. "Different Approaches for Dealing with Social Security." *Journal of Economic Perspectives* 10, No. 3: 55–66.

Gregg, P. and Wadsworth, J. 1996. "It Takes Two: Employment Polarisation in the OECD." CEP Discussion Paper 304, LSE.

Grigg, J. 1978. *Lloyd George: The People's Champion 1902–1911*. London: Eyre Methuen.

Gruber, J. 1994b. "The Incidence of Mandated Maternity Benefits." *American Economic Review* 84: 622–641.

Gruber, J. 1994b. "State-Mandated Benefits and Employer-Related Health Insurance." *Journal of Public Economics* 55: 433–464.

Hahn, F. H. and R. C. O. Matthews. 1964. "The Theory of Economic Growth." *Economic Journal* 74: 779–902.

Hannah, L. 1986. *Inventing Retirement*. Cambridge: Cambridge University Press.

Hansson, P. and M. Henrekson. 1994. "A New Framework for Testing the Effect of Government Spending on Growth and Productivity." *Public Choice* 81: 381–401.

Harris, S. E. 1941. *Economics of Social Security*. New York: McGraw-Hill.

Haveman, R. H. 1985. "Does the Welfare State Increase Welfare?" Inaugural Lecture of Tinbergen Chair, H. E. Stenfert Kroese BV, Leiden.

Heclo, H. 1974. *Modern Social Policies in Britain and Sweden*. New Haven: Yale University Press.

Hedges, L. V. and I. Olkin. 1985. *Statistical Methods for Meta-Analysis*. San Diego: Academic Press.

Henrekson, M, 1996. "Sweden's Relative Economic Performance." *Economic Journal* 106: 1747–1759.

Hills, J. 1993. *The Future of Welfare*. York: Joseph Rowntree Foundation.

Hofferbert R. I. and D. L. Cingranelli. 1996. "Public Policy and Administration: Comparative Policy Analysis." In *A New Handbook of Political Science*, eds. R. E. Goodin and H.-D. Klingemann. Oxford: Oxford University Press.

Hofmann, E. and S. Lambert. 1993. "The 1993 Share Register Survey." *Economic Trends*, no. 480: 124–129.

Holmlund, B. and J. Lindén. 1993. "Job Matching, Temporary Public Employment, and Equilibrium Unemployment." *Journal of Public Economics* 51: 329–343.

Holmlund, B. and P. Lundborg. 1988. "Unemployment Insurance and Union Wage Setting." *Scandinavian Journal of Economics* 90: 161–172.

ILO. 1992. *The Cost of Social Security*. Geneva: ILO.

Ippolito, R. A. 1986. *Pensions, Economics and Public Policy*. Homewood, IL: Dow Jones-Irwin.

Jensen, M. C. and W. H. Meckling. 1976. "Theory of the Firm: Managerial Behavior, Agency Costs and Ownership Structure." *Journal of Finance* 3: 305–360.

Johansen, L. 1982. "Some Notes on Employment and Unemployment with Heterogenous Labour." *Nationaløkonomisk Tidskrift* 120: 102–117. Reprinted in *Collected Works of Leif Johansen*, vol. 1, F. R. Førsund, ed. Amsterdam: North-Holland, 1987.

Johnson, G. and Layard, R. 1986. "The Natural Rate of Unemployment: Explanation and Policy." In *The Handbook of Labor Economics*, vol. 2, eds. O. Ashenfelter and R. Layard. Amsterdam: North-Holland.

Kaldor, N. 1956. "Alternative Theories of Distribution." *Review of Economic Studies* 23: 83–100.

Kaldor, N. 1966. "Marginal Productivity and the Macroeconomic Theories of Distribution." *Review of Economic Studies* 33: 309–319.

Karanassou, M. and D. J. Snower. 1998. "How Labour Market Flexibility Affects Unemployment: Long-Term Implications of the Chain Reaction Theory." *Economic Journal* 108: 832–849.

Kiander, J. 1993. "Endogenous Unemployment Insurance in a Monopoly Union Model When Job Search Matters." *Journal of Public Economics* 52: 101–115.

King, D. 1995. *Actively Seeking Work?* Chicago: University of Chicago Press.

Klevmarken, A. 1994. "Economic Astrology or Empirical Science?" Inaugural Lecture, Department of Economics, Uppsala University, Annual Report 1994, pp. 11–22.

Korpi, W. 1985. "Economic Growth and the Welfare System: Leaky Bucket or Irrigation System?" *European Sociological Review* 1: 97–118.

Korpi, W. 1996. "Eurosclerosis and the Sclerosis of Objectivity." *Economic Journal* 106: 1727–1746.

Kristov, L., P. Lindert, and R. McClelland. 1992. "Pressure Groups and Redistribution." *Journal of Public Economics* 48: 135–163.

Krugman, P. 1994. "Past and Prospective Causes of High Unemployment." In *Reducing Unemployment: Current Issues and Policy Options*. Kansas City: Federal Reserve Bank of Kansas City, pp. 49–80.

Laffont, J.-J. and J. Tirole. 1993. *A Theory of Incentives in Procurement and Regulation*. Cambridge, MA: MIT Press.

Landau, D. L. 1985. "Government Expenditure and Economic Growth in the Developed Countries: 1952–76." *Public Choice* 47: 459–477.

Lane, J.-E. and S. Ersson. 1985. "Political Institutions, Public Policy and Economic Growth." *Scandinavian Political Studies* 9: 19–34.

Layard, R., S. Nickell, and R. Jackman. 1991. *Unemployment*, Oxford University Press, Oxford.

Le Grand, J. 1990. "The State of Welfare." In *The State of Welfare*, ed. J. Hills. Oxford: Clarendon Press.

Levine, R. and D. Renelt. 1992. "A Sensitivity Analysis of Cross-Country Growth Regressions." *American Economic Review* 82: 942–963.

Lindbeck, A. 1981. "Work Disincentives in the Welfare State." *National Ökonomische Gesellschaft Lectures*. Vienna: Manz, pp. 27–76. Reprinted in *The Welfare State*, A. Lindbeck, ed. Aldershot: Edward Elgar.

Lindbeck, A. 1985. "Redistribution Policy and the Expansion of the Public Sector." *Journal of Public Economics* 28: 329–347.

Lindbeck, A. 1993. *Unemployment and Macroeconomics*. Cambridge, MA: MIT Press.

Lindbeck, A. 1995a. "Hazardous Welfare-State Dynamics." *American Economic Review* 85, Papers and Proceedings: 9–15.

Lindbeck, A. 1995b. "Welfare State Disincentives with Endogenous Habits and Norms." *Scandinavian Journal of Economics* 97: 477–494.

Lindbeck, A. 1997. *The Swedish Experiment*. Stockholm: SNS Förlag.

Lindbeck, A., P. Molander, T. Persson, O. Petersson, A. Sandmo, B. Swedenborg, and N. Thygesen. 1993. "Options for Economic and Political Reform in Sweden." *Economic Policy* 17: 219–64.

Lindbeck, A., P. Molander, T. Persson, O. Petersson, A. Sandmo, B. Swedenborg, and N. Thygesen. 1994. *Turning Sweden Around*. Cambridge: MIT Press.

Lindbeck, A. and D. Snower. 1990. "Segmented Labor Markets and Unemployment." Seminar paper 483, IIES, Stockholm.

Lucas, R. E. 1967. "Adjustment Costs and the Theory of Supply." *Journal of Political Economy* 75: 321–334.

Lucas, R. E. 1988. "On the Mechanics of Economic Development." *Journal of Monetary Economics* 22: 3–42.

MacLeod, W. B. and J. Malcomson. 1993. "Wage Premiums and Profit Maximisation in Efficiency Wage Models." *European Economic Review* 37: 1223–1249.

Maddison, A. 1984. "Origins and Impact of the Welfare State, 1883–1983." *Banco Nazionale del Lavoro Quarterly Review*. March: 55–87.

Malinvaud, E. 1985. "Unemployment Insurance." *Geneva Papers on Risk and Insurance* 10, no. 34: 6–22.

Mankiw, N., D. Romer, and D. N. Weil. 1992. "A Contribution to the Empirics of Economic Growth." *Quarterly Journal of Economics* 107: 407–37.

Marris, R. 1964. *The Economic Theory of "Managerial" Capitalism*. London: Macmillan.

Matzner, E. 1996. "The Crisis of the Welfare State." Vienna: Austrian Academy of Sciences.

Mayer, C. 1996. "Corporate Governance, Competition and Performance." OECD Economics Department Working Paper 164, OECD, Paris.

McCallum, J. and A. Blais. 1987. "Government, Special Interest Groups, and Economic Growth." *Public Choice* 54: 3–18.

McDonald, I. M. and R. M. Solow. 1985. "Wages and Employment in a Segmented Labor Market." *Quarterly Journal of Economics* 100: 1115–1141.

McMurrer, D. P. and A. Chasanov. 1995. "Trends in Unemployment Insurance Benefits." *Monthly Labor Review*, September: 30–39.

Ministry of Social Affairs and Employment. 1995. *Unemployment Benefits and Social Assistance in Seven European Countries*. Den Haag: Werkdocumenten 10.

Mitchell, D. 1991. *Income Transfers in Ten Welfare States*. Aldershot: Avebury.

Moore, B. J. 1973. "Some Macroeconomic Consequences of Corporate Equities." *Canadian Journal of Economics* 6: 529–544.

Moore, B. J. 1975. "Equities, Capital Gains, and the Role of Finance in Accumulation." *American Economic Review* 65: 872–886.

Mortensen, D. T. 1989. "The Persistence and Indeterminacy of Unemployment in Search Equilibrium." *Scandinavian Journal of Economics* 91: 347–370.

Mortensen, D. T. and Pissarides, C. A. 1994. "Job Creation and Job Destruction in the Theory of Unemployment." *Review of Economic Studies* 61: 397–415.

Munnell, A. H. 1996. Summary of talk, Jerome Levy Economics Institute of Bard College, Summer 1996, vol. 5, 7–8.

Murray, I. 1996. "Stricter Benefit Regime Scales New Heights." *Working Brief*, no. 77, pp. 18–21 (August/September).

Musgrave, R. A. 1959. *The Theory of Public Finance*. New York: McGraw-Hill.

Musgrave, R. A. 1986. *Public Finance in a Democratic Society*, vol. 2. Brighton: Wheatsheaf.

Musgrave, R. A. and P. B. 1989. *Public Finance in Theory and Practice*, 5th ed. New York: McGraw-Hill.

National Association of Citizens Advice Bureaux. 1994. *Benefit of the Doubt*. London: NACAB.

Nickell, S. J. 1995. *The Performance of Companies*. Oxford: Basil Blackwell.

Nickell, S. J. 1997. "Unemployment and Labor Market Rigidities: Europe versus North America." *Journal of Economic Perspectives* 11, no. 3: 55–74.

Nordström, H. 1992. *Studies in Trade Policy and Economic Growth*. Monograph No. 20, Stockholm: Institute for International Economic Studies.

Odagiri, H. 1981. *The Theory of Growth in a Corporate Economy*. Cambridge: Cambridge University Press.

OECD (Organization for Economic Cooperation and Development). 1991. *Employment Outlook*. Paris: OECD.

OECD. 1992. *Historical Statistics 1960–1990*. Paris: OECD.

OECD. 1995. *Historical Statistics 1960–1993*. Paris: OECD.

OECD. 1994a. *The Jobs Study*. Paris: OECD.

OECD. 1994b. *National Accounts 1960–1992*. Paris: OECD.

OECD. 1996. *Employment Outlook*. Paris: OECD.

OECD. 1997. *Historical Statistics 1960–1995*. Paris: OECD.

Offe, C. 1984. *Contradictions of the Welfare State*. London: Hutchinson.

Olson, M. 1965. *The Logic of Collective Action*. Cambridge, MA: Harvard University Press.

Olson, M. 1995. "The Secular Increase in European Unemployment Rates." *European Economic Review* 39: 593–599.

Oswald, A. J. 1986. "Unemployment Insurance and Labor Contracts under Asymmetric Information." *American Economic Review* 76: 365–377.

Peacock, A. T. 1952. *The Economics of National Insurance*. Edinburgh: Hodge.

Penrose, E. T. 1959. *The Theory of the Growth of the Firm*. Oxford: Basil Blackwell.

Perotti, R. 1993. "Political Equilibrium, Income Distribution, and Growth." *Review of Economic Studies* 60: 755–776.

Persson, T. and G. Tabellini. 1994. "Is Inequality Harmful for Growth?" *American Economic Review* 84: 600–21.

Piketty, T. 1995. "Social Mobility and Redistributive Justice." *Quarterly Journal of Economics* 110: 551–584.

Piore, M. J. 1987. "Historical Perspectives and the Interpretation of Unemployment." *Journal of Economic Literature* 25: 1834–1850.

Pissarides, C. 1985. "Short-Run Equilibrium Dynamics of Unemployment, Vacancies, and Real Wages." *American Economic Review* 75: 676–690.

Pissarides, C. 1990. *Equilibrium Unemployment Theory*. Oxford: Basil Blackwell.

Pissarides, C. 1998. "The Impact of Employment Tax Cuts on Unemployment and Wages." *European Economic Review* 42: 155–183.

Ploeg, F. van der. 1996. "Budgetary Policies, Foreign Indebtedness, the Stock Market, and Economic Growth." *Oxford Economic Papers* 48: 382–396.

Rawls, J. 1971. *A Theory of Justice*. Cambridge, MA: Harvard University Press.

Romer, D. 1996. *Advanced Macroeconomics*. New York: McGraw-Hill.

Romer, P. M. 1986. "Increasing Returns and Long-Run Growth." *Journal of Political Economy* 94: 1002–1037.

Saint-Paul, G. 1992. "Fiscal Policy in an Endogenous Growth Model." *Quarterly Journal of Economics* 107: 1243–59.

Saint-Paul, G. 1994. "High Unemployment from a Political Economy Perspective." Document 94-23, DELTA, Paris.

Saint-Paul, G. 1995. "Some Political Aspects of Unemployment." *European Economic Review* 39: 575–582.

Saint-Paul, G. 1996. *Dual Labor Markets*, Cambridge, MA: MIT Press.

Sala-i-Martin, X. 1992. "Transfers." NBER Working Paper 4186.

Salais, R., N. Baverez, and B. Reynaud. 1986. *L'invention du chômage*. Paris: Presses Universitaires de France.

Samuelson, P. A. 1958. "An Exact Consumption-Loan Model of Interest with or without the Social Contrivance of Money." *Journal of Political Economy* 66: 467–482.

Samuelson, P. A. 1975. "Optimum Social Security in a Life-Cycle Growth Model." *International Economic Review* 16: 531–538.

Sandmo, A. 1991. "Economists and the Welfare State." *European Economic Review* 35: 213–239.

Sandmo, A. 1995. "Social Security and Economic Growth." International Colloquy on "The Nordic Model of Social Security in a European Perspective." In *European Institute of Social Security Yearbook 1994*. Leuven: Acco.

Sass, S. A. and R. K. Triest. eds. 1997. *Social Security Reform*. Federal Reserve Bank of Boston Conference Series No. 41, Boston.

Saunders, P. 1986. "What Can We Learn from International Comparisons of Public Sector Size and Economic Performance?" *European Sociological Review* 2: 52–60.

Schmähl, W. 1995. "Social Security and Competitiveness." In *Social Security Tomorrow: Permanence and Change*. International Social Security Association. Studies and Research No 36, Geneva, 19–28.

Schmid, G., B. Reissert, and G. Bruche. 1992. *Unemployment Insurance and Active Labor Market Policy*. Detroit: Wayne State University Press.

Scott, M. 1989. *A New View of Economic Growth*. Oxford: Oxford University Press.

Sen, A. K. 1977. "Rational Fools: A Critique of the Behavioral Foundations of Economic Theory." *Philosophy and Public Affairs* 6: 317–344.

Shapiro, C. and J. E. Stiglitz. 1984. "Equilibrium Unemployment as a Worker Discipline Device." *American Economic Review* 74: 433–444.

Shleifer, A. and R. W. Vishny. 1986. "Large Shareholders and Corporate Control." *Journal of Political Economy* 94: 461–488.

Siebert, H. 1997. "Labor Market Rigidities: At the Root of Unemployment in Europe." *Journal of Economic Perspectives* 11, no. 3: 37–54.

Singh, A. 1995. "Pension Reform, the Stock Market, Capital Formation and Economic Growth: A Critical Commentary on the World Bank's Proposals." Mimeo, Cambridge.

Sinn, H.-W. 1981. "Die Grenzen des Versicherungsstaates." In *Geld, Banken und Versicherungen*, eds., H. Göppl and R. Henn. Königstein: Athenäum.

Sinn, H.-W. 1987. *Capital Income Taxation and Resource Allocation*. Amsterdam: North-Holland.

Sinn, H.-W. 1990. "Tax Harmonisation or Tax Competition in Europe?" *European Economic Review* 34: 489–504.

Sinn, H.-W. 1995. "A Theory of the Welfare State." *Scandinavian Journal of Economics* 97: 495–526.

Sinn, H.-W. 1996. "Social Insurance, Incentives and Risk Taking." *International Tax and Public Finance* 3: 259–280.

Skocpol, T. 1995. *Social Policy in the United States*. Princeton: Princeton University Press.

Smith, D. 1975. "Public Consumption and Economic Performance." *National Westminster Bank Quarterly Review*. November: 17–30.

Söderström, H. ed., 1994. *Välfärdsland i ofärdstid*. Stockholm: SNS Förlag.

Söderström, L. 1997. "Moral Hazard in the Welfare State." In *Reforming the Welfare State*, ed. H. Giersch. Berlin: Springer, pp. 25–45.

Solow, R. M. 1957. "Technical Change and the Aggregate Production Function." *Review of Economics and Statistics* 39: 312–320.

Solow, R. M. 1971. "Some Implications of Alternative Criteria for the Firm." In *The Corporate Economy*, eds. R. Marris and A. Wood. London: Macmillan, pp. 318–342.

Solow, R. M. 1994. "Perspectives on Growth Theory." *Journal of Economic Perspectives* 8: 45–54.

Stiglitz, J. E. 1986. "Theories of Wage Rigidity." In *Keynes' Economic Legacy*. eds. J. L. Butkiewicz, K. J. Koford, and J. B. Miller. New York: Praeger, 153–206.

Sugden, R. 1989. "Spontaneous Order." *Journal of Economic Perspectives* 3: 85–97.

Tirole, J. 1989. *The Theory of Industrial Organization*. Cambridge, MA: MIT Press.

Turnovsky, S. J. 1996. "Fiscal Policy, Adjustment Costs, and Endogenous Growth." *Oxford Economic Papers* 48: 361–381.

Uzawa, H. 1969. "Time Preference and the Penrose Effect in a Two-Class model of Economic Growth." *Journal of Political Economy* 77: 628–52.

Vickrey, W. 1993. "Today's Task for Economists." *American Economic Review* 83: 1–10.

Wall, H. J. 1995. "Cricket v Baseball as an Engine of Growth." *Royal Economic Society Newsletter* 90 (July): 2–3.

Weede, E. 1986. "Sectoral Reallocation, Distributional Coalitions and the Welfare State as Determinants of Economic Growth Rates in Industrialised Democracies." *European Journal of Political Research* 14: 501–19.

Weede, E. 1991. "The Impact of State Power on Economic Growth Rates in OECD Countries." *Quality and Quantity* 25: 421–38.

Wilensky, H. 1975. *The Welfare State and Equality*. Berkeley: University of California Press.

Wilson, J. Q. 1989. *Bureaucracy: What Government Agencies Do and Why They Do It*. New York: Basic Books.

World Bank. 1994. *Averting the Old Age Crisis*. Washington, D.C.: World Bank.

Young, H. P. 1990. "The Evolution of Conventions." *Econometrica* 61: 57–84.

Index